Endor

"Our lives on earth will shape our eternal existence. In Will You Put Me First? my friend, Dave Gerry, challenges us to view our work as a form of worship—because, as you'll see, what we do matters just as much as who we are!"

John Bevere
Best-selling Author and Minister
Co-founder of Messenger International

"If you've spent time with someone and afterwards remarked, "there was something incredibly different about that person, something that put me at ease, at a sense of great peace," then you've met Dave Gerry. He's a man whose daily life evidences God's Love and Grace. This wonderful book is the life story of a man's faithfulness to God and how God has worked through him. Anyone seeking what God's purpose is in their life will see it clearly through Dave Gerry's example."

Jim Hardy
World Golf Teachers Hall of Fame Member

"Dave Gerry is a friend. Dave is a brilliant businessman. Dave is a wonderful gentleman who would give you the shirt off his back. Dave is a family man. Dave is a man who reveres our Lord."

Craig Culver
Co-Founder, Culver's Restaurant

"By God's grace Dave Gerry showed up in my life at crossroads moments. My life was altered because of those encounters. I will forever be changed. The message in this book, the testimony of a journey with Jesus, will inspire you to seek encounters with the Almighty."

David L. Cook, Ph.D.
Sport and Performance Psychologist
Author/Executive Producer: Seven Days in Utopia

"Dave has been a close friend for many years. He is a gifted storyteller and successful businessman. I have witnessed many of the stories in this book unfold before my eyes. What you're about to read are practical examples of what it can look like to love, serve and obey God in your workplace. I'm thankful for the impact Dave has had in my life and I am certain your life will be impacted positively by this book as well."

Stan Utley
PGA Tour Winner, renowned short game instructor

"There are people you meet you'll never forget – not because they are personally impressive, but spiritually impressive! Dave's stories give you a glimpse into the power of discerning and obeying in fearless humility...a power that makes a difference both in the church and in the marketplace."

Wayne Schmidt
General Superintendent, The Wesleyan Church

"Dave is one of my heroes of the faith! He demonstrated how a faithful businessman can have an impact in a community. ... What most impressed me about Dave is that he was willing to simply obey God, whatever the cost."

Dave Konkol
Outreach Pastor, First Free Church, Onalaska, WI

"Will You Put Me First will inspire you to settle for nothing less than God's absolute best for your life. Dave's humble and yet radical obedience to Holy Spirit in the marketplace, in the "real world," proves God is every bit as interested in working outside the four walls of the local church as He is inside. Read this book and go after your God-filled destiny."

Chris Conrad
Regional Superintendent, The Wesleyan Church

"Dave's heart is one like our Heavenly Father's, full of compassion and love. Being in Dave's presence is such a blessing. I walk away from every interaction with Dave feeling like I have been with someone who had been with Jesus. Dave inspires my heart to be more on fire for Jesus."

Ryan Bibb
Lead Pastor, Radiant Life Church, Sturgis, MI

"Dave is a unique servant, led by the Spirit, that God uses to open the eyes, ears, and hearts of leaders longing for more of God. I highly recommend taking the time to let his stories invite you into your next step of Kingdom work and ministry."

Dr. Brian Bennett
Lead Pastor, Pathway Church, Vero Beach, FL
(Author: Go Now and Be the Church: Becoming an Overflowing Community)

"[Dave] is a voice of both wisdom and experience when it comes to navigating change at a church as well as in the marketplace. I feel stronger as a person of faith when Dave Gerry is in my presence."

Wes Dupin
Founder and Former Lead Pastor, Daybreak Church, Hudsonville, MI

"Dave is a marketplace leader who's built his career and reputation on his relationship with Jesus. He has made a profound impact on his community by investing in the souls of marketplace leaders and pastors alike."

David Doerner
Teaching Pastor, Frontline Community Church, Grand Rapids, MI

"Without a doubt, one thing [Dave] has never been about is "Dave Gerry ministry, clout, reputation or brand." He is about Jesus, period, and that is why I admire him so much!"

Garth Heckman
CEO The David Alliance; Senior Pastor, HillSpring Church, New Prague, MN

"Dave's life gives image and story that will inspire many in their marketplace work to live for Jesus!"

Peter Yoshonis
Lead Pastor, All Shores Wesleyan Church, Spring Lake, MI

"I've been blessed to meet with Dave on multiple occasions and he has a true anointing in his life. He's the real deal."

Steve Jones
Lead Pastor, LifeChange Church, Dorr, MI

*"As a pastor for more than 40 years, I've recognized that Dave's integrity & humility is **unparalleled** and his generosity is **unprecedented**."*

Glenn Smith
Pastor, Co-Founder Shepherd 2 Shepherd Ministry

"As a successful businessman and Spirit-filled leader, Dave Gerry has uncovered the importance of building the bridge between the marketplace and the pulpit. His life is a powerful example of God's desire to use the marketplace as a platform to advance His Kingdom. Dave's life paints a picture of what the world looks like when the Church sends out anointed business leaders to shine the light of Christ in every sphere of life."

Allison and Chandler Stevens
High School Ministry Directors, Life Stream Church, West MI

WILL YOU PUT ME FIRST?

True stories from a Christian businessman in Madison, WI.
From arson to multimillion-dollar deals.
Whose Kingdom are you building?

Dave Gerry
With Jessie Gerry Czech

Copyright 2023 © Dave Gerry

All rights reserved.

No part of this book may be reproduced, stored in a retrieval system, or transmitted by any means, electronic, mechanical, photocopying, recording, or otherwise, without written permission from the author.

ISBN (Paperback): 979-8-9878693-5-2
ISBN (eBook): 979-8-9878693-4-5

"God's Kingdom is not just **inside a building**. God is God and His Kingdom is all across the earth. His Kingdom is being established within our neighborhoods, our schools, our cities and our government. And what He's doing right now is waking up His body because He wants to move in our midst in new ways! That means your work as a student, homemaker, banker, plumber, teacher, bus driver, HR worker, dentist, lawyer, administrative assistant, CEO, athlete, politician, janitor, daycare worker … is <u>holy</u>. That's right, when done unto the Lord and operating in your unique gifts and abilities: Your Work Is Holy."

Table of Contents

Acknowledgement xi
Introduction xiii

Chapter 1: Health Club 1
Chapter 2: Elizabeth House 19
Chapter 3: Crusade 37
Chapter 4: Bryan Peterson 57
Chapter 5: Mike Kuglitsch 63
Chapter 6: Whose Kingdom? 69
Chapter 7: Identity 75
Chapter 8: Interns 83
Chapter 9: Epilogue 93

Appendix A: How to Share the Gospel 97
Appendix B: Hearing the Voice of God 109
Appendix C: A Note To Pastors 115

Acknowledgement

I would like to take a moment and say thank you to my precious daughter, Jessie Gerry Czech. Walking with her through this lifetime has been more than I could have ever expected as a father. We walked together for miles on the golf course as she played professionally and I carried her bag. As a caddie, I learned that you walk with and sometimes just ahead of your player, but your only goal is to encourage and help carry the load. Thank you this time, Jessie, for carrying the load and walking with and going before me in writing this book.

Love,
Dad

Introduction

January 2001. Jamaica.

"If you were really holy, you would quit your jobs and become missionaries in Africa."

Five hundred CEOs began to squirm as those words echoed across the auditorium. The silence was his answer as we waited for the keynote speaker to talk. The conference that day was full of ambitious and talented people who loved God and wanted to serve Him. Many of whom, if pressed, would admit to feeling guilty about working a job outside the walls of a church.

It was so quiet you could have heard a pin drop. After allowing us to sit in the tension of that comment for several seconds, the speaker, Henry Blackaby, finally broke the silence: "That's what you all think... isn't it? You think, *Maybe I'm a little greedy and just want to make money*? You think that if you were really holy, you'd leave your job and become a missionary."

The posture of the crowd and the sound of squeaking chairs across the room made it obvious that was what many believed.

"That is a lie!" Henry exclaimed. "If you were *really* holy, you would do *exactly* what Jesus Christ died for you to do and you would function *exactly* where He's placed you to function."

I'm telling you, something shattered when I heard those words. It was the first time I had heard someone else say the very thing I had carried in my heart for a long time.

I knew deep down that God had given me a gift to be in business and that my work in the marketplace as a health club CEO was exactly what God created me to do. But I wasn't <u>always</u> this confident. I remember twenty years prior, in my early 20s, wondering whether or not I should become a pastor. Becoming a pastor was the only model I had seen of how to love and serve God *in a job*. During this time, I spent a lot of time with my senior pastor – Warren Heckman. He took me under his wing and allowed me to be a part of many things he was involved in. I loved hanging out with him, but quickly discovered I wasn't wired like him. Our giftings were unalike. I was made for something different and sensed my destiny would be realized in the business world. Functioning in that arena came so *naturally* to me. The Lord began to teach me that I was gifted to run the **same race** as a pastor or a missionary – **but in a different lane**. It's like we were both athletes, but gifted to play different sports.

Picture this: You are an athlete, too. You know you were born to compete, and the one sport you've seen played is basketball. Seeing basketball players train, practice, and play in games awakens something in your soul. You want to be a part of the A team, so you sign up for tryouts.

Now you're on the court, surrounded by other players during a scrimmage. As your teammates dribble, pass and shoot with precision and finesse, you feel clumsy and out of place. Every time you try to plant your foot and make a hard cut under the basket, your footing slides out from under you. It's embarrassing and sometimes even painful. While those around you are making no-look passes using their keen peripheral vision, you find yourself unable to see the whole court. You frequently commit fouls because you can't seem to maneuver around without knocking people over. You're not angry or trying to hurt anyone, you just can't help it. Your teammates are patient, but you're causing more harm than good. You feel out of place and in the way. None of this makes sense. As an athlete, you thought joining the basketball team would be a natural fit, but your role on this team isn't clear for some reason. Frustrated and confused, you double up your effort and determine to do a better job. Your intentions are good, but your efforts leave you more *exhausted* and *discouraged* than ever. (This is how I felt when I tried to do the work Pastor Heckman was doing. I just didn't fit.)

Then it happens. You get subbed out. You're tired and frustrated, so the break is a welcome relief. As you make your way to an open seat on the bench, you see the head coach coming down from the bleachers. He's coming towards you. *This will not end well*, you think to yourself as you grab a towel to wipe the sweat from your face. Certain you'll get cut from the roster before the season even begins, you brace yourself for what's about to happen. To your surprise, he seems enthusiastic to talk to you.

"You are an incredible athlete," he says with the kind of conviction only a seasoned head coach can convey. Turning your head to see if there's another player behind you, you're shocked to find he actually meant to say that to you. He extends his hand to help you up, "Come here, I've got to show you something." As you rise from the bench, he leads you over to a part of the gym you haven't seen before. Moving closer, you catch a glimpse of your reflection in the window of the gymnasium. The glance catches you off guard as you see something you were not expecting. You have a helmet on. There are big pads on your shoulders. Your shoes are not rubber-soled sneakers, but cleats. As your eyes strain to look out the window, you see it. Another athlete dressed just like you.

Without words, the basketball coach motions with an affirming nod to keep moving closer. He reaches in front of you and swings open the back door. For the first time in your life, you see it: A football field. A shot of adrenaline rushes through your veins.

"You weren't made to play basketball, son. You're a football player if I've ever seen one, and I'd love nothing more than to see you compete out there."

As you step outside the four walls of the gymnasium, your cleats sink into the grass. Instinctively, you know you're going to be able to run faster than you have ever run before. No more slipping, no more holding back. As you move closer to the action, you see a team full of athletes wearing equipment just like you. Out here on the football field, all the equipment you have on has a specific purpose. Your heart begins to pound, and, at that moment, you are certain this is where you belong. The football coach jogs over to you and puts his arm around your shoulder, "I'm glad you are here. The team needs you. Let's go."

Here's the thing: The hundreds of business people in the auditorium listening to Henry Blackaby that day weren't made to be pastors or foreign missionaries (basketball players) – and most of you reading this book weren't either. You're football players. And you're not second best. You were made to be children of the living God. Designed with intention and purpose. Created to seek and obey the will of your Father in heaven. Equipped to go out and bring the lost into His Kingdom. And do you know what? All that "football equipment" you have on is going to be used to break down strongholds in your region. There are too many people out there – people who God loves, people Jesus died to save – who aren't going to walk into a church. But whether they know it yet or not, they are desperately searching for the truth. And He has positioned *you* in a specific arena to reach them.

You.

With your unique giftings and abilities. The passions and skills the Lord has strategically given you to use in your sphere of influence. In your city. In your family. In your workplace. Think about this: God will move in your city, inside AND outside the four walls of the church, when you use the gifts and abilities he has uniquely given to you.

So let's break down the box we sometimes put God in and erase the line between "sacred" and "secular." Stop wasting time and energy trying to fit a mold you weren't created to be in. Let's move from being spectators to participating in the work the Lord is doing across the earth! As you read the stories in this book, my prayer for you is that the weight of shame – and the feeling of being less holy, less significant, less important, or less valuable – would dissipate forever as you see, *you are not second best*. Your position is vitally important to the Kingdom. Nearly four decades of work in the marketplace has taught me that advancing the Kingdom of God will require all of us. Basketball players and football players. Working together. As one body. With one mission. For the honor and the glory of Jesus' name. It's time to get in the game.

CHAPTER 1

Health Club

1985. Madison, WI.

6:55 pm. I was so nervous. Although I was twenty-five years old, not knowing what I was going to say had me feeling much more like a kid. I leaned against the back wall and watched as 75 employees walked past me to find their seats. I was about to become their new manager, but since my promotion came with a transfer from a different location, they were all strangers to me. After my third visit to the bathroom, it was almost time for the meeting to begin.

The hallway leading back to the aerobics studio was lined with windows, so I could see a room alive with energy as I made my way back into the studio one final time – each step filled with excitement and nerves.

Just before turning the corner to enter in, I had this sense – somewhere between my pounding chest and belly button. It felt like a question, or maybe even an invitation: **"Will you put Me first?"**

I wanted to chalk it up to nerves and move on with the evening. But for some reason, I couldn't. It's hard to describe. Somehow, I knew it was God. At that moment, I didn't know how to respond.

What does that even look like to put You first? I was comfortable with the idea of *"putting God first"* on a Sunday morning at 10 am. But this was the real world of business. This was my moment to prove to my bosses they had made the right decision in promoting me. This was my moment to make a good first impression on a room full of people I was about to lead. This was *my moment.*

As I struggled to refocus, I caught the eye of my boss across the room. He nodded to me, signaling it was time to get things started. As he approached the stage to kick off the meeting, the prompt in my gut returned: **"Will you put Me first?"**

My mind was racing as the company president began to speak. After a few brief introductory words, he turned to me and said, "… and now I'd like to introduce Dave Gerry." Still unsure of what I was going to say, I approached the stage wrestling with what felt like an invitation from the Lord. I thought about the verse that says, "In everything you do, put God first, and He will direct you and crown your efforts with success."[1] In *everything you do, put God first…* I reached to receive the microphone from my boss. One more time, that sense returned: **"Will you put Me first?"**

I took a deep breath as uncomfortable obedience ensued.

"You know what, I'm not really sure how to do this… but before I even begin, I just want to take a minute and put God first." I proceeded to duck my head down and say the Lord's Prayer. It felt like it took *forever!* As I prayed, I could hear a few of the body-builder guys in the back chuckling. I was certain they thought I was a nut job. However, I was encouraged to hear a few of the women in the front row join me in prayer.

"… for Yours is the Kingdom and the Power and the Glory, forever and ever. Amen." I lifted my head, wiping the sweat from my brow with a slightly shaky hand. Nothing happened – outwardly. But inside… something had taken place that is hard to describe.

---

[1] Proverbs 3:6 TLB

I *knew* that I had *pleased* God. Plain and simple. It wasn't like I had *earned* anything – it's just that I knew my slightly awkward act of obedience meant more to Him than I could imagine. I was convinced from that moment on things would not be the same and that my daily approach to business and life moving forward would be this: Remain sensitive to the Holy Spirit and what He wants to do…then obey.

Let me rewind about one year from that meeting in the aerobics studio. With the fitness craze sweeping across America in the 1980s, I wanted in on the action. Big hair, bright colors, and parachute pants filled exercise facilities throughout the country. Demand for health clubs was growing, so I left my stereo sales job and began selling memberships at a health club. I wanted to be all-in, so even though I was close to graduating from the University of Wisconsin, I dropped out. I never did end up getting my degree, but that's a story for another time.

My first sales job for this new employer led me to Clearwater, Florida… and let me tell you, it didn't take long for this Wisconsin kid to say yes to that offer. This was a temporary assignment as I was tasked to pre-sell memberships out of a trailer while the club I worked for built a new facility on-site. Like many entry-level jobs, I ended up doing much more than my job description. When I wasn't actively selling, I was involved in helping landscape the new facility. Shoveling and spreading piles of mulch in the Florida heat had me wondering if dropping out of college was the right decision. For whatever reason, I distinctly remember a moment when I paused, rested my hands on my shovel, and looked up to the sky. "It can't get lower than this in this industry," I thought. My dreams were so much bigger than this, but sometimes the days of small beginnings are just a proving ground to show how badly you want it.

As I demonstrated to my boss I could handle the work they were giving me, that's when my promotion to manager came. The

Clearwater club I had done pre-sales in was open and I was heading back to Wisconsin.

I started to find my rhythm as a manager in the months after that aerobics studio meeting. The staff I led were achieving their goals and our member base was growing quickly. We were crushing it. Things were happening quickly and I was on the fast track to the successful business career I had dreamed about. Unfortunately, that fast track was about to come to an abrupt stop as I caught wind of some questionable behavior higher up in our company. My boss argued the lavish purchases were for the business, but I knew better.

My Dad was always a trusted confidant and sounding board for me, so I called him to talk through the circumstances. After listening for a while, he encouraged me to step away and distance myself from the company. That would have been much easier if I had a degree to fall back on or at least a little more money in my savings account. But I knew deep down, he was right. After much consideration, I made the incredibly difficult decision to resign. As hard as that was, it was that decision which solidified something inside of me that had been stirring for a long time – the desire to be my own boss. I decided to move back down to Florida and begin exploring the idea of starting my own health club.

It wasn't long before the shady decisions being made at the top had finally taken their toll. The health club company I had worked for went bankrupt. As the dust settled from the news of their bankruptcy back in Madison, the kind of opportunity I had been on the lookout for presented itself. The club they had built just one year earlier on the East Side of Madison was available. I knew I needed to act quickly, so I packed up my earthly possessions – a tv and two trash bags filled with my clothes – and drove from Florida back to Wisconsin.

Sometimes in your life, moving back and forth between places and jobs seems to have no rhythm or reason. The trips back and forth between Florida and Wisconsin always seemed purposeful, yet this was a case where the job didn't seem to pan out. Something else pretty cool was in the works, though. While in Jacksonville, I met an amazing woman named Jean, who later became my wife.

When I arrived back in Wisconsin, I went over to meet the bankrupt club's landlord. I found out I wasn't the only one with my eye on this club. The "Goliath" of the fitness industry in the 70's and 80's, *Bally's International*, was interested in making an offer. They owned and operated 350 clubs across the United States, and with one location already in Madison, they wanted to take over this East Side club too. In fact, they had plans to fly someone in from London the following week to look at the interior of the existing club. I needed to act quickly, so I called the only guy I knew who might be able to help me out – Don Evans.

Don had been a lifelong friend of my Dad's. His banking savvy and real estate investments made him respected in Madison. I invited Don and my Dad to lunch and over burgers, shared my new idea. My Dad managed a NAPA auto parts store and didn't make much money. He was in no position to invest financially in this new endeavor, but he provided something that could not be bought: credibility. As we sat around the table that day, Dad looked at Don and said, "Don, if David says he's going to do it, I'm telling you – he will do it." That was enough for Don. He agreed to loan me the money I needed to take over the health club. I couldn't believe it!

My Dad, Ted Gerry, Sr., outside the NAPA auto parts store he managed. Madison, WI.

Knowing Bally's had someone coming to scout out the club in just a few days, I scheduled a meeting with Don and the landlord as soon as possible.

When Don and I walked into that meeting to negotiate a deal two days later, the landlord of the property said, "You set me up, Dave!" I wasn't sure what he meant. Opening his arms wide in Don's direction, he said, "I've known this guy for 35 years!" As they greeted one another, I took my seat – relieved to see things were off to a great start.

That relief was short-lived as I learned Bally's had made an offer on the club before actually visiting it. I thought we missed our opportunity, but Don didn't seem phased.

Not one to beat around the bush, Don looked the landlord square in the eyes and said, "I think we want to do this."

Without hesitation, the landlord replied, "If you're in on this Don, I'm in too."

I guess I didn't need to pitch him my business plan.

The landlord proceeded to call the head of Bally's International right in front of me. "I've got a young local guy and his partner from Madison who want this club," he said. I don't know if the guy from Bally's thought the landlord was messing with him – trying to raise the rent or something – but he held his ground. The original offer from Bally's was final. The landlord could take it or leave it. "Ok, I'll call you right back," the landlord said as he hung up the phone. He looked back over at Don and said, "Are you serious? You want to do this deal?" Don stood up, reached across the desk, and shook his hand, "Yes."

I knew the significance of that handshake. Though contracts had yet to be signed, the deal was done. This club was going to be ours.

The landlord immediately called Bally's International back. "Thank you very much for your offer," he said. "I just made a deal with someone else. Have a great day."

Click.

That was it.

My heart was pounding out of my chest. So loud, I was sure Don could hear it sitting next to me. I had never written a check over $1,000 in my life, so when it came time to write the $73,000 check to cover the first and last month's rent plus the security deposit, I was just hoping to get all the numbers in the right order. My hand was shaking as Don watched over my shoulder. Don picked up the check and scanned it as if to say, *"I'm backing you on this, but I'm going to be watching to see that you do this right."*

He handed it over to the landlord, "Well, here you go."

Looking back at me, he pointed his finger at my chest: "I hope you write a lot more of these someday…" he paused and, with a wry smile continued, "… but I hope they are to you and me." This was an investment for Don and he expected a good return. I knew this opportunity was rare and I didn't want to let him down.

The loan from Don was just enough to get me in the door. While Don provided the upfront capital, he was not in a position to continue funding things. That meant it was on me to immediately start securing memberships to generate income or we would fail. I will never forget the first day I opened the door for business. July 17, 1987 – 5:30 am. My heart was in my throat as I unlocked the door that morning. *The Princeton Club* was officially open and there was no turning back.

Those early days were a grind. Long days doing all we could to sell just *One. More. Membership.* I hired a few people to get things rolling. My Dad and brother Ted each worked the night shift for a while. My longtime friend Scott had recently graduated as a CPA and came on board to handle our accounting. Each of us had to wear many different hats. From selling memberships to cleaning locker rooms behind the scenes – and everything in between – we did whatever it took. We were committed to excellence and made sure our members knew it.

I remember several **years** of feeling exhilarated and terrified on a daily basis. *Welcome to being an entrepreneur.* It was a rush. It took many years with this first club before we were established enough to expand our operation. During that time…

WE WORKED HARD.

I mean, we worked *really* hard.

It was five long years before we were profitable. Five years of lying awake some nights. Five years of wondering if we were going to make it. Five years of reassuring my wife on our Sunday evening walk that I would do whatever it took to provide for her and our young family. And then, as we began to turn the corner to profitability, it was another four years before we felt ready to expand.

Nine years into owning the East Side Princeton Club, the fitness scene in Madison was booming. People were flocking to join health clubs, and our company was growing. The Princeton Club name was well-known and reliable on that side of town, but it was time to expand further. We had our sights set on taking over an existing health club location 15 miles away on the west side of Madison. The landlords and the management team operating this location were all in their early 70s and didn't want to be in the fitness business much longer. I expressed my interest not in competing with them, but in giving them an opportunity to exit the scene by buying them out. Once I explained to the landlords that Don Evans was still involved as my partner, they were ready to move ahead with negotiations. People <u>really liked</u> that guy.

I was excited about the prospect of owning the premier health club on each side of town and felt like the Lord was opening the door to this opportunity. This would be the biggest acquisition our growing company had ever made – just over a one million dollar purchase. After several meetings to negotiate a deal, the day to sign the lease finally arrived. I was a few strokes of a pen away from a dream come true. Everyone in the city of Madison would soon know about the Princeton Club.

Signing day was going to be the biggest day of my career and I was pumped. As I came off the elevator on the second floor of the building, somewhere between my chest and belly button, I heard that voice I had heard years earlier. But this time, it was loud and clear:

"STOP."

This wasn't an invitation – it was more like a command. *Am I losing my mind?* I thought to myself as the elevator door closed behind me. *I mean c'mon, what in the world am I supposed to do?* I wondered if the devil was trying to keep me from my destiny. I could see the board room. Papers on the table. Bankers, lawyers, and businessmen waiting for me. All that was needed was my signature. My dream was so close to being reality.

What would *you* do?

Let me tell you what I *wanted* to do. I wanted to say, "Ehh, that was just the tacos I ate the night before," and sign those papers. That couldn't have been the Lord... *right?* I mean, this wasn't in church on Sunday morning. People were paid a whole bunch of money to get these documents together, and a lot of time had gone into preparing for this moment. This was serious stuff.

But here's the thing: If you want to follow Jesus Christ, you have to obey him. Period. Implicitly. Every single time. Even if it's uncomfortable. Even if it makes no sense in our earthly economy. Even if a boardroom of people thinks you're nuts.

As I slowly approached the conference room, I had a choice: Pretend like I heard nothing and go ahead with my plan to sign the contract that awaited me ... or obey. There was no time to seek the opinion of others. This was between me and God. I was battling internally between what I *wanted* to do and what I *knew* in my spirit He wanted me to do.

In one desperate last attempt, I crossed the threshold of the door and pleaded with the Lord under my breath: *God, if this isn't you, I need to know right now. Please.*

Nothing.

My stomach churned and I felt nauseous. There were so many questions and doubts running through my mind. I didn't have any answers, but I knew what I needed to do.

Immediately upon entering the boardroom, I took a deep breath and said, "This isn't going to make any of you very happy..." The tone of the room stiffened. To say this was one of the most uncomfortable moments of my life is an understatement. I continued, "I know we have spent a lot of time and money putting this deal together and I don't really know how to explain this. All I can say is that I pray about things before I do them, and for some reason, I'm just not supposed to do this deal right now. I don't know why, and I am so sorry."

If. Looks. Could. Kill. I'm telling you, I wouldn't be alive any longer. All around the room, blank stares of disbelief and confusion were looking back at me. One glance, in particular, pierced my heart – Don Evans'. My trusted business partner and mentor. He looked as though I had just punched him in the stomach. After all he had done to help set me up for this moment, the last thing I wanted to do was let him down.

Embarrassed, I assured those gathered in the room that I would cover their legal fees leading up to that day. There were no words left to say. I felt like I had just blown the biggest opportunity of my career, and in the process, probably destroyed my credibility in the business community. Apologizing again, I slowly backed my way out of the room. As I made my way down the hall to the elevator, humiliation and confusion flooded my mind. *Why would God have led me to this moment, only to tell me to STOP just short of the finish line?* I felt disillusioned. Hurt. Angry. Irritated. Sad. Frustrated. Confused. The only thing I had to cling to was the fact that *to the best of my understanding*, I had obeyed. And sometimes, simple obedience needs to be enough – even when you don't have all the answers.

Will You Put Me First?

It is in these moments – the moments where we want something *so badly* we can taste it – that we truly see what is in our hearts. When the Lord asks you to surrender something of great value, that is when things get real. I wish I could tell you that everything made sense the next morning, but I wrestled with these questions in my heart for many months.

One of the hardest things for me to do following such a massive disappointment was to show up and work hard every day back at the East Side Princeton Club. But I did, and over time, the sting of the abrupt ending to this deal started to fade. Though, I still had questions that I wanted God to answer for me.

I will never forget what happened next. After a full year had gone by, I received a phone call while at work in my office. It was Don Evans.

"David, are you sitting down?" he asked. It was 1999, and my office phone had a cord attached to it… of course I was sitting down. Don was quite a reserved man, but even he couldn't mask the excitement in his voice.

"You are not going to believe what just happened. The landlords of the west side health club just left my office. They want to get out of the health club business. David, they are going to **hand you the keys** to the west side club."

I tried to process what he just said, but it didn't make any sense.

He continued, "They only want to be the landlords and said that if we come over and sign the papers to take over the operation, *the club is ours*. All the memberships, equipment, stereo systems – everything in the existing club, they're just *giving* it to us.

"What?!" I said, "What about the million dollars we settled on last year?"

"They don't want our money, David. They are literally going to hand you the keys to the front door."

What in the world? Time seemed to stand still as I sat in silence. I couldn't find the words to respond. A year had gone by since that crushing day I believed the Lord had told me to "**STOP.**" A year of uncertainty, with no next steps. Every day was laced with confusion and not knowing the *why* behind the Lord's direction.

That year felt like a generation.

As I pondered what was unfolding before me, suddenly, I remembered the moment I was about to be introduced as a manager for the first time. A 25-year-old kid, just wanting to do a great job. That simple invitation from the Lord, "**Will you put me first?**" This memory from over a decade ago was fresh in my mind. The platform on which I had stood that day was in the aerobics studio of the very first health club I had managed. The same health club that had later gone bankrupt. Which just happened to be the same health club God had told me not to purchase for one million dollars the previous year. And now was the *same health club* that I had *just been offered the keys to!* I was so blown away by who my Father in heaven is.

"David?" Don's voice on the phone snapped me back into the moment. With tears in my eyes, I whispered back, "Ok. Yeah. Let's do it."

I have no recollection of what I said to Don after that. What happened was so far beyond anything I could have imagined in my wildest dreams. I was overwhelmed and just sat there thanking and praising God.

Only God could have orchestrated something like that, and only God could have produced what came next. When we took over that west side location, people came flooding in to buy memberships. We did eight months' worth of business in the first 30 days we were open! It was really something special.

As a company, we have persisted in our commitment to excellence over the last 35 years. We started with 2,000 members, and today, the Princeton Club has over 50,000 active members. We have continued to expand and operate 11 health clubs in the upper Midwest. All glory to God.

And Don's initial $73,000 investment? That made him a millionaire, but here's the coolest part: **Don gave his life to Christ** before his death in 2000… and that is something worth exceedingly more than any investment could ever be.

Main Workout Floor. Princeton Club West, Madison, WI

Exterior. Princeton Club West, Madison, WI

Rooftop Soccer Field. Princeton Club West, Madison, WI

Outdoor Pool. Loves Park, IL

Will You Put Me First?

NO SWEAT.

College dropout, 34, builds Princeton Club into national leader.

By Melanie Radzicki McManus

David Gerry is a fair pick for king of Madison's fitness scene. He's president of the profitable Princeton Club, one of the largest health clubs in the U.S. with over 10,000 members. He's currently building a new $4 million, 52,000-square-foot facility, and has plans on the drawing board for another $3.5 million in expansions. And he's a mere 34 years old.

Gerry (pronounced Gary), a Madison native, credits his amazing success to

David Gerry proudly oversees a model of the new Princeton Club, which will sport an aluminum high-tech look exterior. A football-field sized workout area, olympic pool and 200 parking stalls are other features of the planned facility.

CHAPTER 2

Elizabeth House

2002. Madison, WI.

In addition to operating The Princeton Club over the years, we have worked to develop commercial real estate surrounding the health clubs. The retail space we created is leased to tenants in a wide variety of ventures. Things such as a physical therapy clinic, a shoe store, and a bike shop are among a few of our tenants.

In 2001, I took a portion of one of these retail spaces next to the East Side Princeton Club and dedicated it as a 'House of Prayer.' It wasn't a church but rather a space for anyone who wanted to come and worship, pray and sit in the presence of the Lord. It truly was a special place, **right in the midst of the marketplace**, where it felt as though God was there waiting for you when you entered. After a few months, the number of people coming in and out of this space increased, and I knew I would need to expand the 'House of Prayer'.

There was a daycare on the land next to us – just outside the back door of the House of Prayer. If I acquired that building, I could easily add square footage to the House of Prayer space. Here's how that meeting went:

"If I were to find land and build you a brand-new building, would you trade me for the building you are currently in?" I asked the owner.

NOT the way to start negotiating a business transaction, by the way.

Our businesses had neighbored one another for a long time, so he knew me well enough to know I wasn't pulling his leg. The offer was too good not to explore, so a couple of days later, he sent his son to join me in searching for potential locations. Of all the sites we saw that day, the one that stood out was just a couple of miles away on McArthur Road.

I called the real estate agent listed on the site and scheduled a meeting with him for the following day. Going into the meeting, I had a strong sense from the Lord to pay close attention. As we talked, I learned that I knew both the family that currently owned the land as well as their attorney. The agent couldn't help me further as he no longer had the listing. I thanked him for his time and left. As I got to my car, I called the attorney representing the family. I had worked closely with him a year earlier to purchase the land where we had built the latest Princeton Club. He answered my call right away. I explained I was interested in this piece of land on McArthur Road that he represented and when I asked if he'd sell it to me, he said yes.

Over the next 24 hours I prayed about going ahead with purchasing this two-acre parcel. As I waited, I sensed the Lord say, **"Take the land."** Remember, not an audible voice, but a *knowing* somewhere between my chest and belly button.

All I needed to relocate the daycare was two acres of land. This was back in the day when we used fax machines, so the attorney faxed me the information along with an offer to purchase. He also included the information about a three-acre lot adjacent to the one

I was interested in – *just in case* I might like to buy both. This land was a great location that sat on a major highway running through the city of Madison and now I had the inside track to purchase it. Again, I took things before the Lord and asked for discernment about how to proceed. This time as I waited, I had no sense about what to do with that additional three-acre piece. I decided to sign the contract for the two acres and pass on the three-acre parcel.

What happened next still gives me chills. Not long after the fax went through, I received a call from the attorney:

"I've talked to the family and they have accepted your offer," he said with hesitation in his voice, "…but there is something they insisted I tell you. They know you're probably not going to like what I'm about to say, and if you want to cancel the deal, it's ok with them."

Not exactly what you want to hear from an attorney in regard to a deal you have just signed.

He went on, "The other three-acre piece adjacent to the one you're buying had a medical center looking at it, and they have decided to purchase it. But here's the thing Dave, it's not just a medical center, it's an **abortion clinic**."

I couldn't believe what I just heard. "You've got to be kidding me," I said, astounded.

I need to pause right here and say something before I continue on with this story. I recognize the subject of abortion can bring up many different responses in people's hearts. Regret, anger, confusion, and pain. Statistics say that one in three of you reading this story right now will have had your life impacted by abortion. Whether you have had an abortion yourself, encouraged someone else to have one, or closely know someone who has – please hear me: There is no shame or condemnation in the words I am saying. The Lord offers forgiveness and freedom to each of us. Maybe you felt trapped. Scared. Alone. Uninformed. And you reasoned the only option before you was to end the life of your unborn child.

It is for precisely that reason I am so passionate about the story I am about to share with you. Not only do we serve a God who is incredibly gracious, loving, and forgiving, we also need to have alternatives that enable women to have the ability and opportunity to choose life. So any passion, frustration, or righteous indignation conveyed in the words I share with you is <u>not</u> directed at you. Trust me, I am very aware that I need God's grace every bit as much as anyone else, and my heart is full of compassion and mercy when I think about the situations those impacted by abortion find themselves in. The story that follows is about a *solution* and that is why it matters so much to me to share with you what God did.

The attorney knew I needed some time to process this new information and told me to give him a call the next day. I hung up the phone, absolutely stunned. I had never seen something so black and white. Here I was, trying to relocate a daycare and the potential neighbor was going to be an abortion clinic?! I couldn't handle the thought of that. It's hard for me to convey the intensity that erupted inside of me in these moments. Something was rising inside my spirit that I had not felt before. It was less about my opinion about what should happen and more that I was feeling the Father heart of God. I felt like a warrior. I knew this abortion clinic was not supposed to buy this land.

When I got home later that day, I explained to my wife, Jean, what had taken place. She was just as shocked as I was and we decided to pray together right there. I remember taking her hand in the kitchen and together asking the Lord to show us what he wanted to do in this situation. It was after that time of prayer with my wife that we both knew what needed to be done.

I called the attorney back the next day and found that though a deal was in the works, a *contract had not yet been signed* by the abortion clinic on the three-acre piece. It was one of those moments in my life where I had a very clear impression of what to do next. The contract to buy the additional three acres of land was *sitting in my fax machine*. But before I could do anything with it, I needed to see if the financing was in place. I called the bank and they wanted 50% for a down payment. That was a number I could not afford. After discussing with the man at the bank what was going to be built on the three acres if I did not purchase the land, he asked if I could swing 20% down. Though this would be a massive financial investment for our family, I quickly said yes. I don't make decisions of that magnitude impulsively, but because of the word I had from the Lord and because of the unity and peace I had with my wife in prayer, I knew it was the right move. In a matter of moments, I had signed and faxed the contract to the attorney, who then brought it to the landlord. The deal was done and the land had been taken away from the abortion clinic.

This was one of those times in my life where obedience in action was the necessary response to the word God had spoken. It required an immediate adjustment to my life. And it was a costly one – both in faith and financially. With a signature, the land was bought out from under the abortion clinic! And with the same signature, I now owned five acres of land that I had to make payments on for the next thirty years. I didn't know how I was going to make that work logistically. The only hope I could cling to was that I had done what I thought the Lord asked me to do.

As all kinds of questions raced through my mind, I sought the Lord in prayer. One person's name kept coming to my attention: Liz Osborn. Liz is a longtime friend of our family. It had been quite some time since I had seen her last, but for some reason, she was the only person I could think of as I prayed. One morning, before I had the chance to reach out to Liz, my wife and I went for coffee. Jean and I had been praying together about what the next step with this land would be. We also asked a few close friends to join us in prayer.

I opened the door to Cool Beans coffee shop, and sitting in the back room were Liz Osborn and **two of the friends I had asked**

to pray for us – Sam and Jennifer Dharam! Knowing I would be far too distracted to sit up front sipping coffee, we made our way toward the back room. As we approached their table, Sam looked at me and said, "Dave, I think this is a God moment."

I want Liz to tell you a little of what was happening in her world in the moments prior to our arrival...

Liz: "I remember the moment we saw Dave and Jean walk in. Sam said to me, "That's the guy you need to talk to." I was the executive director of Care Net Pregnancy Center of Dane County and had just been released by my board of directors to go out and find land on the east side of Madison. We were looking to build a residential maternity home for pregnant women who might otherwise be homeless or in unsafe housing. At that time, all we could offer young women in need were small maternity homes in rural places. These homes, while safe and stable, were challenging for our residents because there was no public transportation to Madison and therefore limited access to jobs and schools. Our desire was to help set our young women and their families up for success.

The vision of building a residential maternity home in Madison had been stirring inside of me for some time. As I started to speak to others, I realized that God had inspired the same vision in them as well: A home where residents would have more access to employment opportunities, education, public transportation, and community. A home in the heart of Madison. The reason I was at the coffee shop that day with the Dharams was to ask them to pray with me about where this new home should be. I had been looking at various properties, but every site our board had considered up until that point had come up empty."

Dave: They invited Jean and me to sit with them, and Liz shared with us what the board of directors had commissioned her to look for. She also told us that for some time she had wanted to contact me and ask for financial help, but every time she asked the Lord, she didn't feel His release to do so. When I heard that, I <u>knew</u> this was a woman who feared the Lord. Because of all that had recently taken place (and how Liz had been brought to mind several times in prayer) the sentence *"I know where your land is!"* flew out of my mouth. Immediately I thought: *Oh no, what did I just say?! I can't believe I just said that out loud.* I'm sure Jean was having the same thought.

Pause here with me in this moment: I had recently signed a contract to pay for five acres of land. Care Net Dane County is a faith-based, non-profit organization. They can't afford that land. I am committed to thirty years of payments – I can't really afford that land either! *Did what I just blurt out to Liz mean I was supposed to pay for the land myself and give it away to them?* Clearly, I did not have a plan in place – but something deep down inside of me knew this was right.

We concluded the impromptu meeting in the coffee shop, knowing something significant was taking place. Not wanting to waste time, Jean and I planned to host Liz and a group of people in our home for dessert to learn more about Care Net. Our living room was filled with people that night, so I sat on the floor in front of the TV. Liz spoke briefly and then played a video about residential maternity homes that had been built in other places across the country. What I watched that night stirred something in my soul and I began to quietly weep. I knew it was the Lord and I knew I was to be a part of what He was doing through Care Net.

In the coming weeks, the Care Net "Steering Committee" members met frequently to plan and pray. It was a unique and exciting time, but still stressful for me. I remained committed but was unclear on how this was going to work financially. As I continued to seek the Lord, I finally heard His solution. I sensed his still, small voice:

"Sell half the land for twice what you paid for it."

Now, I say I heard His solution because this was not *my* solution. I had been in real estate long enough to know that is not how it works. I had just purchased the land at market price. It would take years for the land value to increase enough to be sold at twice the purchased price. It was simply impossible. It made no sense, but I was starting to sense God's repeated leading to obey – even when I did not understand. I responded to him: "Okay God, if that's what you want to do, you'll have to bring the buyer."

And then I waited. Fortunately for me, I didn't have to wait long.

Three days later, the phone rang, and it was a man named Owen McCluster. Owen represented a company called Community Living Alliance (CLA).

He said, "Mr. Gerry, I heard that you just bought some land on MacArthur Road."

There was never even a sign up, so I have no clue how he knew that.

"Would you be interested in selling any of it?"

"How much land are you looking for?" I asked.

"Two and a half acres," he said.

That got my attention as that was half of the property I had just purchased.

"Let's get together to talk," I said.

I like to talk face-to-face, so the next day I met Owen in his office. It was a unique meeting in that I didn't do any negotiating. This was hard for the salesman in me, but I knew God had clearly spoken: **"Sell half the land for twice what you paid for it."** And that was my intention.

After introductions, I got straight to the point, *"Here's what I'm going to do: I'm going to sell half the land for twice what I paid. I paid $3.25 sq/ft and I'm going to sell it for $6.50 sq/ft."*

Most people who have been around real estate for more than two seconds would have called me crazy, but Owen didn't seem to flinch.

Now, I want to share the details of the numbers here because it will help you appreciate what God did. One acre of land equals 43,560 square feet. If you have any desire to be involved in commercial real estate, memorize that number. I had purchased five acres of land (217,800 square feet) for $3.25/ square foot which means I paid $707,850. CLA was interested in buying half of the land I owned. A two-and-a-half acre piece which, based on the price I just paid for it, was valued at $353,925. Over the following few weeks, I met a few more times with Owen to discuss what CLA was looking for and if we could settle on a price. Before long, an offer came from CLA for $650,000. If you're doing the math, that was $296,075 **more** than I had just paid for that piece of the land. It was an incredible offer. But it was also $57,850 less than what **"twice what I paid"** for it would be. It was unheard of in real estate to receive an offer that much higher than market value so quickly after purchasing. There are not many ways to make a $296,075 profit in such a short period of time. My mind raced considering what could be done with that kind of money. Personally, it was huge and would certainly take a lot of stress off my plate! But even if I were to donate it – that kind of cash could really help others.

If I passed on this deal, not only would I be the laughing stock of the businessmen in Madison for having turned down an instant $296,075 profit, but I would still be solely responsible for making payments on the land for many, *many* years. I wrestled with whether or not I was crazy to consider passing on this offer. *Was I just splitting hairs?* I mean, $650,000 is an amazing offer, and *really close* to $707,850.

My desire to be completely obedient to what God had prompted was at war with the reality of the lucrative offer that sat in front of me. Put yourself in my shoes for a moment and be honest – what would you do in that situation? For me, this is where the rubber met the road.

As I considered my options, the bottom line was this: God said to **sell half the land for twice what I paid for it**. And $650,000 is not that, $707,850 is.

I went back to Owen's office hoping to clarify, "*I might have confused you, but I meant $6.50/ sq. ft – not $650,000.*"

"Oh, we knew that," he said, "it's just our counteroffer. This is what we can afford, so this is what we want to do."

I took a deep breath. "*Owen, I'm sorry, but I'm going to have to pass on that offer.*"

That sentence sounded as bad coming out of my mouth as I thought it would. And then he said something that sounded even worse: "Well, thank you. We're getting pretty close to Christmas and there are some other pieces of land we are looking at. Let's talk after the holidays."

After thanking him politely, I walked out. I wanted to cry. It was one week before Christmas and I had just passed on an amazing deal. I was stuck with this land and these payments and starting to wonder if I had heard God correctly. Not only that, but I had a group of people who wanted land for a Pregnancy Care Center, and they were getting their hopes up that I would make that land available to them. While I was tempted to allow stress to reign supreme that Christmas, I knew I had to trust that the Holy Spirit was up to something and that He was inviting me to simply trust Him. As the temptation to doubt crept in, I was surprised when I received another call from Owen just a few days later on Christmas Eve.

"Mr. Gerry, I hope I didn't offend you earlier this week," he said. "Our board went out and looked at all the other pieces of land we were considering. The only one we want to buy is the one that you own. If it's ok with you, by three o'clock this afternoon, I'll have a courier personally deliver the **full-price offer** of $707,850 to your home."

I. Was. Stunned.

I couldn't say yes fast enough. This seemed too good to be true. But this is the honest truth: after buying five acres of land, I turned around and **sold half the land for twice what I paid for it**. This meant that the entire parcel was **completely paid for** – debt free. Because of the wisdom and brilliance of God, I was then able to call up Liz Osborn and say, *"Remember in the coffee shop when I blurted out that I knew where your land was? ... it's on McArthur Road – and I'd like to donate it to you. It's **completely paid for**.*

God is amazing.

A campaign began to raise the $2.2 million needed for construction. It was striking how the community came together in support of this project. The money came pouring in from private donors and churches of all denominations.

I remember Liz telling me the story about when they had around $500,000 yet to raise, she received an email while in the office one afternoon. A couple, who wanted no fanfare, simply offered to pay off the remaining debt. They wrote a check for just under $500k!

By 2004 as the construction was underway, 43 different churches across many denominations were involved in raising support. My friend, the late Bishop Robert C. Morlino even authorized a collection in parishes throughout the Diocese of Madison. When interviewed, he said, "We must do more. This is the bedrock principle of our faith and more importantly, it proclaims the truth that all human life is precious to God and only He can decide when life is spent. We share this view with other Christians. Our Christian brothers and sisters have asked for our help. I want to give it to them."

The unity demonstrated to accomplish an undertaking like this was incredible. There was a team of 6 Master's degree students from UW Madison who worked together to design the brochure for the Elizabeth House. Three were pro-life and three were pro-choice!

My longtime friend and current business partner, Mark Landgraf – who owned Landgraf Construction, Inc. at the time – built the Elizabeth House. But Mark and his team did much more than the build itself. Landgraf Construction, Inc. donated $30,000 in pre-design estimating, local approvals, and submittals; $45,000 in overhead and profit expenses; 20% of labor costs for framing and finish work; as well as their personal time and talent to the construction of the Elizabeth House. Mark went out of his way to personally discuss the project with each subcontractor, asking them to give in kind to this project with no minimal markup or donation. In total, $300,000 was donated in the form of materials, labor, and equipment rental by the many companies involved in construction.

One of my favorite details as construction began on the Elizabeth House was the stone stacking ceremony that took place. What the Lord was orchestrating to create the Elizabeth House was miraculous. It was about what God was doing, not what one person or one church could do on their own. The unity was unprecedented and this "stone stacking" ceremony was simply a physical representation of that. Pastors from many different denominations and leaders from various organizations each brought a literal stone to this dedication. The stones were piled up outside the front door of the Elizabeth House and remain there to this day. As future generations stop to ask why they are there, this story of God's plan and faithfulness will continue to be told.

Will You Put Me First?

The Gerry Family at the stone-stacking ceremony.
Elizabeth House, Madison, WI.

The net result of this unified push to support young women in need was this: The entire building was paid off in four years! That is unheard of. Hundreds of people from all walks of life teamed up for one common goal: To build a safe, supportive, and loving home for women struggling with unplanned pregnancies. A home with staff that becomes family. A home that welcomes and cares for mom and baby before and after birth. A home that is free of charge.

In 2005, the Elizabeth House opened. Under Liz's leadership, the staff, volunteers, local churches, and community joined together and have since served a total of 286 women and babies. With three sets of twins, there have been **137 babies born** ... and counting! In addition to housing an average of six or seven moms per year, Care Net Pregnancy Center's Elizabeth House program has a state-of-the-art medical facility on site. They offer STI Testing and treatment for women and expedited partner treatment to help stem the rising tide of sexually transmitted infections. Pregnancy testing, ultrasounds, childbirth, and parenting classes, as well as healthy relationship education, are all offered **free of charge** to those in need.

Care Net Pregnancy Center's Elizabeth House. Madison, WI.

While assistance for an unplanned pregnancy is often focused on the mother of the baby, a father's role in the life of a child is crucial too. For those men who desire to be a part of their baby's life, a program called "Being Dad" is available to help equip them to become engaged and involved fathers. In a day and age where many Dads are absent, this is an amazing gift to children and a much-needed resource to facilitate healthy co-parenting.

But that's not the end – it gets better! After selling 2.5 acres to CLA, the other 2.5 acres were donated to Care Net – but they only needed 1.25 acres to build what would come to be known as the Elizabeth House. In considering what to do with the remaining 1.25 acres, Liz and I met to discuss some options. We talked about how that extra land had the potential to be used to create an ongoing revenue stream that could be funneled back into the ministry. The idea of building an apartment complex came up... where Care Net would own the land and lease it to a management company. But not just any apartment complex – affordable workforce housing where successful graduates from the Elizabeth House could be more independent and live next door. They could still take advantage of all the resources Care Net had to offer: classes, a computer room, laundry, and they could even come over for Sunday night dinner. This would allow them to take the necessary steps toward independence, while still having support from the community that had already been walking with them on their journey. Eagle Harbor Apartments was built on this land, and the long-term vision for an ongoing revenue stream is still alive today.

Since Eagle Harbor Apartments were built as affordable workforce housing, that means six of the apartment units are available at 30% of the county median income. These savings reduce the financial responsibility of the women who have newly graduated from the Elizabeth House and are embarking on their careers. As they do so, they move into paying 40% of the county median income and incrementally on up until they are 100% able to be on their own and afford full rent.

There's one final piece to cap this story that is just incredible. Before any part of this story took place, I was in a prayer meeting with several pastors from the Madison area. There was a man there from Malaysia named Dr. Colin Gordon. Dr. Gordon is gifted in prophecy and after praying for all of the pastors, he asked if he could pray for me. As he began to pray, he said, "I see it! I see the house! It's two stories, and upstairs are many bedrooms on both sides. Angels are escorting young women into those rooms. And downstairs, it looks to me like it's a medical clinic." The layout for the Elizabeth House is such that the upstairs level is where the bedrooms are located, while downstairs is where the medical clinic exists. Dr. Gordon prayed this prayer without having any idea of what the Lord was in the process of doing – not to mention before there was ever a plan drawn for the Elizabeth House. You can't make this stuff up! There is no way to look at this story without recognizing the hand of God in every detail.

Every year, as a birthday gift, I receive a letter in the mail with pictures of each of the precious babies who were born and began their lives in the Elizabeth House that year. It is one of the most significant and powerful gifts I receive each year. This home continues to be a beacon of hope in our community to this day.

You might be wondering what ever happened to the daycare I was hoping to relocate from the beginning of this story. We ended up expanding our retail units surrounding the East Side Princeton Club and built a bigger space to move the House of Prayer. The daycare that neighbored us ended up staying in their location for many more years. Do you know what's neat though? Lighthouse Kids Early Learning Center is in the same building as Eagle Harbor Apartments on the land next door to the Elizabeth House. Turns out a daycare was built on that land after all.

Check out https://www.elizabethhousedane.org/ if you're interested in learning more!

A footnote about Liz Osborn – a woman I am proud to call my friend. There is a powerful piece to her story you need to hear…

Liz: "Abortion became legal in 1973. I myself worked as an abortion nurse in the late 70's. It was the sexual revolution and it seemed as though "love" was free – but it sure cost me dearly. Not only did I assist in countless abortions, but I also had one myself, a decision I've regretted countless times. Then in 1983, I came to my senses. God was speaking to me, and I listened. Before I knew it, I found myself whispering in a client's ear, "You don't have to go through with this." And that's been my message ever since. To those who are post-abortive: if God can forgive someone like me

– who participated in thousands of abortions and had one myself – please know that you can be forgiven and set free too."

For those hurting from an abortion, rachelsvineyard.org is a helpful resource (with a toll-free national hotline).

CHAPTER 3

Crusade

1999. Madison, WI.

"You didn't leave the gas line to your grill on..." the police officer said. Lowering his voice so the kids couldn't hear, he continued, "This was arson."

His words resounded in my ears. Jean and I looked at one another. A new wave of adrenaline swept over my body as my mind began to race. This was no accident. Someone just tried to start my house on fire in the middle of the night.

By 3 am, we were back inside the house. After tucking the kids in bed, the questioning began. Sitting at our kitchen table, the officer started in: "Have you been threatened lately? Is there anyone who may be upset with you?"

"No," I said.

This didn't seem like a normal checklist of questions following a house fire. This was an interrogation.

The officer continued to press, "Have you received any threats or unusual offhand comments?"

"No."

"Do you have a girlfriend? Have you said or done anything to make someone's husband jealous or angry?"

"No."

"Do you gamble... have any gambling debts?"

"No."

They were trying to get to the bottom of why someone would try to burn our house down. I also wanted an answer, but by the end of the inquisition, we were left with more questions than anything else. The officers had their notes and told us they'd be in touch. As they left, they assured us the house was safe from the fire – but we all knew this was not a closed case. Thankfully, the kids were getting a few more hours of sleep before having to head to school later that morning. It wasn't likely Jean and I were going to get any more shut-eye that night, so we brewed a pot of coffee and sat in silence – contemplating what had just taken place. As the first morning light began to break through the kitchen window, I was wracking my brain trying to come up with a reason why something like this would have happened.

Suddenly, the thought of the contract I had signed the day before flashed in my mind. *Was there a correlation between what I had just agreed to and this arson attempt?*

Let me back up a little bit here. A month earlier, while at work one afternoon, I received a phone call from my pastor – Warren Heckman. He wanted to know if he could have a couple of guys come over and visit with me about the potential for a crusade[2] in Madison.

---

[2] Crusades were large gatherings, typically held in sports stadiums and arenas around the country from 1950 to the early 2000s. Christians invited their non-Christian friends to hear powerful preaching and testimonies. A speaker shared the Good News of Jesus and God's incredible love for all people. Non-Christians were invited to believe in Jesus, and many did. Hundreds of thousands of lives were transformed through these crusades.

I scheduled an appointment with the two gentlemen for the following week and was prepared to do what most people meeting with me hoped I would do: write a check to support the cause. I loved the idea of an event in my hometown that would share the gospel with thousands of people. As my meeting with Lowell and Chet got underway, I was surprised to learn they weren't here to ask me for money. Lowell was an evangelist who had been preaching at crusade events for four decades. Chet was his assistant, and together they were looking for someone local to chair the event. They were in my office that day because Pastor Heckman had suggested... *me*. I did not feel particularly qualified to accept such a position, and quite frankly was a bit taken aback by their request. I was a *businessman*, not a *pastor*.

Guys, I'm honored that you would even think to ask me to do something like this. Can I have some time to pray about it and get back to you?

"Absolutely."

As I began to ask the Lord what he wanted my role in this crusade to be, I made plans to drive to Lowell Lundstroms's church in Lakeville, MN. I wanted to sit in the back of a service and hear him preach a message. On the morning I had prepared to leave, I suddenly had a strong sense that I wasn't supposed to go that day. I wasn't sure why, but I've learned to heed those impressions from the Lord. Instead, my family and I went to church together. It began as a typical Sunday but was about to take an extraordinary turn. As the service wrapped up, I decided to make my way to the front of the church to be prayed for.

A pastor in our church for many years, Bernie Norland, was up there with his wife, Donna. Pastor Norland had known my family for decades. My father had great respect for him, and I wanted him to pray for me as I tried to navigate whether or not I was to chair this crusade. Jean and I went forward, and I began to explain to the Norlands what Lowell and Chet had invited me to be a part of.

"I'd love for you to pray for me because, quite frankly, I don't know if this is something I'm supposed to do or not," I said. "I know enough to know that if this is not something the Lord is leading me to pursue, I don't want anything to do with it."

Jean was standing next to me. Donna took one of my hands, Bernie the other. The *moment* Pastor Norland touched my hand he started *weeping*. At that same moment, I felt a weight come down on top of me and I was instantly crushed to the ground. It was like nothing I had ever experienced. There I was, in a heap after buckling to the ground in the presence of the Lord. Donna and Bernie had knelt down to continue praying for me, both in tears. For just the second time in my adult life, I was crying too. The first was when I held my daughter right after she was born. I really wasn't sure what was happening, but I knew this was the Lord. I was a strong, healthy 37-year-old man unable to stand because I felt the presence of God in a way I had never experienced before. This was new to me, but I knew I didn't make that happen. To this day, it remains one of my most powerful encounters with the Lord. At that moment, I knew something significant was taking place; I knew I was supposed to say yes to chairing the crusade.

After accepting the invitation to chair the event, I decided to commit to taking time every afternoon to seek the Lord. I came home from my office at the health club for a designated amount of time. I sat in a small room attached to our bedroom that overlooked the backyard. The windows on three sides allowed ample natural light in while also giving us a great view of the conservancy our yard bordered. We didn't have much as far as furniture in this room – just one chair. This room quickly became my place to go and spend undistracted time with the Lord. My family affectionately referred to it as the "prayer room." Sometimes I prayed, sometimes I read the Word, and sometimes I just sat at His feet and waited on the Father. The point was I didn't have an agenda. I just wanted to hear from Him. It was in these moments that God began to give me a strategy for this city-wide crusade.

The first impression I had was the idea of an event before the crusade to draw local pastors *together*. A "huddle" of sorts where we could all begin to unify around this vision of reaching those who hadn't heard the Good News of Jesus.

You've heard me say this before, but let me reiterate: I have never heard God audibly. It has always been that *sense or knowing* somewhere between my chest and belly button. As I sat on the floor in my prayer room one afternoon, I heard His familiar voice:

"Reggie White."

It was out of the blue, but as I thought about it, it made sense that a name like Reggie White could be the perfect draw to bring a bunch of pastors together. If there is anything that Wisconsinites are unified in, it's their love of the Green Bay Packers! White played a total of 15 years in the NFL for 3 different teams: The Philadelphia Eagles, Carolina Panthers, and (most importantly) the Green Bay Packers. Not only was Reggie one of the most decorated players in the history of the NFL, but he was also an ordained evangelical minister. Known as "the Minister of Defense", White was a force to be reckoned with on and off the field. With 198 career sacks, Reggie White ranks 2nd on the NFL career sacks list.

He'd be perfect! Here's the problem: At the time, Reggie was a big deal in the world of football, and it wasn't going to be easy to get in touch with him. For those born after the 90s, think JJ Watt, Aaron Rodgers, Russell Wilson or Patrick Mahomes. Today you can tweet @ them, and *maybe* they'll see you and communicate. Probably not. But in 1999, even that wasn't an option. I did what any modern 1999 business guy would do: Dial up America Online to connect to the World Wide Web. In a world before high speed internet, 5G data and instant access to anything on the internet…there was dial up. You'd start by powering up your massive computer – that was most certainly glued to your desk and in no way portable. Then, over the course of the next few minutes, you'd endure the high-pitched screeching and dial tone noises as the computer worked to connect to the internet. So there I was, staring at my computer screen wondering how to get ahold of Reggie White. Though Google was formally incorporated in 1998, it had yet to become the number one search engine. Hard to believe, right? I probably typed my question into a search engine like "Yahoo" or "Ask Jeeves" instead: *How to get ahold of the Green Bay Packers.*" Then I tried the Yellow Pages. The yellow pages were… never mind. Bottom line: this was going nowhere.

My attempted research left me no closer to contacting this guy than when I began. But I knew this was something the Lord was leading me to do, so I surrendered the whole idea to him. I knew that if Reggie was the guy that God wanted to use to gather the pastors together, He was going to have to make the introduction.

At work the next day, I mentioned to my brother Ted the failed attempts at contacting Reggie in hopes of inviting him to Madison.

"Really?" Ted asked. "Sondra Wood knows Reggie White's agent."

Are you kidding me?

Sondra was the worship leader at Ted's church, as well as the choir teacher at my kids' school. I was shocked that my brother actually knew someone who knew someone that could get ahold of Reggie. I had known of Sondra but had yet to formally meet her, so I left the health club and went straight to Abundant Life Christian School. Sondra wasn't there that afternoon, so I left a note asking her to call me.

The next day at work, my phone rang. It was Sondra. I was so excited that I launched right into explaining what I was hoping to do. She stopped me, "Your brother already called and told me, so I called my friend Vaso right away – he is Reggie White's agent."

I could sense the excitement in her voice as she continued, "When Vaso called me back after speaking with Reggie about this, he shared that the first thing Reggie said to him was, 'That's the Lord. I need a couple of days to pray about it and verify, but I'm telling you right now, I'm supposed to do that.'"

I could hardly believe what I was hearing. Not only had Reggie been contacted and invited to come to speak, but he was on board! Only God could orchestrate things this brilliantly. A few days later, I received a phone call explaining that after taking a couple of days to pray about it, Reggie was absolutely in. He was going to come to Madison to draw together a group of pastors in preparation for a region-wide crusade. Things were being set into motion and the "huddle" was about to be called.

This "huddle" was going to take shape as a luncheon. Considering the fact that Reggie was going to be a big draw we would need a large space. Of all the venues the city of Madison had to offer, the Monona Terrace Convention Center was one of the best. This 67-million-dollar public convention center had just opened in 1997. It was in the heart of downtown Madison, overlooking both Lake Monona and the dome of our state capital.

I met with an event coordinator at the Monona Terrace to ask about hosting a luncheon. The conversation went something like this:

"How many people will be in attendance?" they asked.

Well, at this point, I have no idea, I responded.

We were off to a great start.

They showed me different options and when we came across a room that overlooked the lake and held about three hundred people, I said, "That's great, let's do that one."

"Ok, do you have any idea what kind of catering you'd like?" they asked.

I had an answer for this one: *Yes. It's not going to be chicken. I want it to be a first-class event – steak and shrimp.* This luncheon was going to be done with excellence. It was not going to be a pot-luck picnic. I wanted to honor the Lord and what he was doing by making each detail exceptional.

After some more time discussing logistics, they were able to generate a commitment contract for me to sign. I remember taking a deep breath before I signed the paper as I considered the significance of the cost of an event like this. I had a house payment, a car payment, and two young kids at home. This was a bold act of obedient faith – an invitation to trust Him. Yet I never felt like this was my idea or event. Every step along the way felt like I was operating more as an agent or steward on behalf of the Lord. Which, by the way, doesn't mean there weren't mildly terrifying moments along this journey.

I sure hope it's not just me sitting in this room eating steak and shrimp, I thought as I went ahead and signed.

It was later that evening, as my whole family was fast asleep, that we were suddenly awakened by a loud *whoosh!* My eyes opened and I shot out of bed. Our bedroom was on the second floor and connected to the prayer room. With windows on all sides of the prayer room, I could see flames stretching across our backyard all the way up to the house. In the pitch black of night, things were lit up like it was the middle of the day. We immediately rushed out of our room to grab the kids and dog. Jean was dialing 911 as we all ran down the stairs, making our way out the front door as quickly as possible. It all happened in a matter of moments, but my adrenaline kicked into high gear as I thought about the location of that inferno.

On the ground level under the prayer room, we had a three-season porch with a grill inside. A grill with a gas line attached to it. A grill where I had cooked dinner the night before. As our family rushed out of the house, all I could think was that I had somehow forgotten to ensure the gas line was off. In the midst of the rush to get out of the house, I forgot the car keys. As Jean and the kids made their way to the driveway, I ran back into the house to grab the keys off the kitchen table. I had my head ducked down because I was afraid the house was going to blow up at any second.

In no time, our street was filled with fire engines, police cars, and an ambulance. It was amazing how quickly they had all arrived on the scene. My kids held tightly to our golden retriever in the back seat, the flash of red lights illuminating their faces. Eyes wide, observing the drama unfold, I assured them we were a safe distance away and that everything would be okay.

As the firefighters jumped out of their truck, they began running to the back of the house where the flames were. I yelled out the window of my car, *"Don't go back there! The gas line is lit. It's going to blow up!"* I couldn't stand the thought of anyone being injured or killed because I had forgotten to turn the grill off. The warning didn't stop them from doing their job. My heart was pounding as I waited. Moments later, to my surprise, it seemed like everything was under control. They had quelled the flames. *"Thank you, God,"* I whispered under my breath. Considering I was fully prepared for my home to be blown off the planet, I was quite relieved as an officer came walking down the street toward our vehicle.

"You didn't leave the gas line to your grill on..." the police officer said.

A mixture of relief and confusion settled over me. I was relieved to know I wasn't the one responsible for creating such a chaotic and dangerous scenario; and yet confused, wondering what in the world was happening. Lowering his voice so the kids couldn't hear, the officer uttered 3 words I never expected, "This was arson."

He continued, "We're going to make sure everything is safe and I'll come back over once that's done. Then you can all get back in your house, but once you get the kids settled, we need to talk."

Thank you, officer.

After the whole emergency response team had completed their safety checks, they assured us it was safe to re-enter our home. We took some time to reassure the kids everything was all right. After praying with each of them, we tucked them into their beds.

Then, Jean and I went back to the kitchen to meet with the officer. After what felt like an inquisition, we wrapped up our conversation with more questions than when we had begun. The officers had their notes and told us they'd be in touch. They assured us that the house was safe from the fire, but I could tell they were uneasy about why it was started in the first place. They left, and I went to inspect the damage. The smell of smoke lingered in the air and charred grass littered the yard.

I stepped into the prayer room and flipped on the flood light to look out across the backyard. I was startled to see an arc burned in the grass. A straight line was burned from the woods behind our house right up to this arc. The arc was in the shape of a semicircle right around where our house began. Right around where my prayer room was located. It was at that moment, I sensed the protection and sovereign authority of the Lord. It was like God was showing me how He had drawn, with His mighty hand of protection, a line where He would allow the enemy to go no closer. He protected my family and my home. It was as if God was saying, "I allowed the enemy this close, but he **will not** cross that line."

Over the coming days, the authorities conducted investigations into this arson attempt. They brought in dogs and arson investigators. They found a gas can and a watch, but no substantial footprints or fingerprints. There was no conclusive evidence and to this day, nothing has ever been solved. The only damage done to our home was some melted plastic siding and screens around our porch. And the lines burned into our grass. But I'm glad those lines were there. For me, it was a tangible reminder of how the Lord had protected us.

Fire damage at our home following the arson attack.

I told Pastor Heckman what had happened that night, and he asked a team of people to pray for us. Their prayers were almost tangible to me and my family as the peace of God transcended our human understanding. My kids were in 1st and 3rd grades when this happened and they didn't have any issues sleeping following the fire. They weren't fearful in the night and that alone was a testament to the Lord's protection.

Over the following weeks, we began to have prayer meetings in our home. A number of people from various churches in the city came together and we asked the Lord for direction and guidance. This was uncharted territory for all of us, and the Lord stretched each of us as we learned to trust him in a new way. During one of those prayer meetings, my brother, Ted, shared with me a scripture he felt like God had given him for the event as he was praying: **Isaiah 55.** He had his Bible open to that passage and read it to me, "Come, all you who are thirsty, come to the waters; and you who have no money, come, buy and eat! Come, buy wine and milk without money and without cost."[3] My spirit knew immediately this was a word from the Lord. This event was not going to cost *anything* to those attending. We used Isaiah 55 as a template for the crusade and if an idea or plan didn't align with that scripture, we didn't do it. Period. There were many details yet to figure out, but one thing was clear: there was not to be a penny taken for this event.

Here's where that got challenging. I can't stress how strongly I knew this wasn't **my** event. I was just a business guy and had never aspired to lead a crusade. But for whatever reason, the Lord had invited me into this position and my only aim was to obey his lead. Meetings with pastors around the city and with Lowell Lundstrom's Ministry team became a regular part of my schedule. This meant entering some unfamiliar and intimidating environments.

Many people who had been doing this crusade thing much longer than me: pastors, elders, people a generation older – insisted on a different model. The things they were saying made a lot of sense but weren't lining up with the passage I *knew* was to be the template for this event. Ted and I respectfully heard them out, but we both knew deep down that this event was to convey the following message: Salvation is a free gift and you don't need money to receive it.

Even Lowell Lundstrom's ministry model was shaken by the idea of having all the expenses covered. Lowell was a man's man – reminded me of a rugged cowboy. Tough. Strong… and with a heart that burned to share the love of Christ with the world. My kids still joke about the way he greeted them whenever he saw them at the crusade – a tight squeeze on the neck that made their shoulders shrug. He was a seasoned minister and for forty years had been traveling from town to town as an evangelist. The number of people this man led to Christ was staggering! His experience led him

---

[3] Isaiah 55:1 NIV

to develop a formula for when he entered a city – which was wisdom on his part. His team created deadlines, appointed intercessors to pray, and required a certain number of people and churches to be involved. He had learned what was required to have a successful event. But for us to assert there would be no fundraisers, no entry fee, and no offerings taken was a foreign idea to him. *Who was I to insist on doing things differently?* Remember, I was just the health club guy who had **never done this before**. But here's the thing: *I knew that I knew* that God had given me Isaiah 55 as a blueprint and following His lead was the **only** thing that mattered to me.

Eventually, I convinced Lowell I believed the Lord was asking me to fund the event, but there was one stipulation. It was common for Lowell to ask the crowd for a "free will offering" that would be used to fund the next Crusade. Great idea. But again, not God's idea for this event. I remember looking Lowell square in the eyes and saying, "*When you have the mic in your hands, if you ask for an offering in the middle of this crusade, I'm not paying for this event. If you don't take an offering, I'll pay for 100%.*" And I meant it. That was our understanding and thankfully, he agreed. We came together under one common goal: seeing people come to know Christ. It was clear that the essence of this event was this: 'Salvation is a free gift. It costs you nothing. Come freely.'

Reggie White Luncheon

With Lowell and his team on board, the next step was gathering pastors around the Madison area. The luncheon with Reggie was a very special day. The excitement was tangible as *hundreds* of pastors filled the Monona Terrace Convention Center in a room overlooking the lake. There were over sixty different churches represented from Madison and the surrounding areas. **Sixty!** Denominational barriers were being smashed. It was the first time in my life I had seen that kind of unity in the body of Christ.

We took the kids out of school that day to be part of the event. It has always been important to Jean and me to make sure our kids are a part of the things God is inviting us to do. They have grown up experiencing God in many ways, and it's fun to hear them as adults share stories of their memories of these times. **Always make room for your kids**. Take the time to bring them along as you journey with the Lord. Sometimes it might be messy or inconvenient, but I promise you, it will always be worth it. Your family is your first ministry. They will be your lasting legacy. You will bear more fruit by investing in your family than you ever could on your own. Generations will be impacted for eternity.

Reggie White with my wife, Jean, and me. Madison, WI.

We sat as a family having lunch that day with Reggie and his agent, Vaso. My son, Teddy, was trying on Reggie's Super Bowl ring. Reggie was 6' 5" 300lbs, and Teddy could fit three fingers inside the ring. It was really cool to watch.

These types of events always have an agenda – a detailed breakdown of speakers, timing, and content. We didn't have that. I knew that made the stress level rise a bit, but I wanted this to be led by the Holy Spirit, and not by people. While the pastors were having lunch and getting to know one another, I shared my plan with Reggie and Vaso. I told them I'd like to simply ask the Holy Spirit who should speak next and what should happen. I'm pretty sure they were starting to think I was a little crazy – I can't blame them. But they said they were on board.

As lunch was wrapping up, I experienced something I never had before. I had been a born-again, Spirit-filled Christian for most of my life, but it wasn't until this day that I began to understand what the word 'anointing' meant. The best way I can describe what happened to me next was that I felt very heavy and weighted down, yet simultaneously joyous and excited. I could barely get my forehead off the table where we were sitting. I'm not joking. I sensed the presence of God so powerfully that my face was on the table. I didn't know what was happening to me or why I felt this way. Vaso looked across the table at me and said, "Dude, the anointing of God on you is so heavy, I've never seen anything like this. You can't even get your head off the table."

I couldn't have defined the word 'anointing,' but I remember thinking to myself, *"If that's what this is, this is amazing... this is so cool."*

Our original thought was to have Vaso introduce Reggie. But as the time came for them to go up, Vaso said he wanted me to introduce Reggie instead. He recognized God was doing something. I didn't have any plan about what I would say to this room full of pastors, and I certainly didn't have Reggie's resume memorized.

But you know what? At that moment, none of that mattered. As I walked up to introduce this giant of a man, I felt an authority come from the Lord for me to speak. Before I said a word about Reggie, the following words came pouring out of me:

"Have you ever been in a football stadium and seen a team warming up before a big game? Before the game begins, you have the offense down on this end – the defense down over here," I said, motioning with my hands from one side to the other. *"Over here you have the quarterback with a couple of wide receivers running patterns. The team is spread out, all over the field, preparing for their role in the game."*

I could see the crowd of pastors engaged with what I was saying. They were about to hear from one of the all-time NFL greats, so they were excited about football.

I went on, *"But there comes a moment, right before the game starts where a whistle is blown..."* If I would have had a whistle at that moment, I would have blown it so loud! *"...the whistle blows, and the referee says, "Gentlemen, it's time for the game to start."*

The cadence in my voice quickened as I knew these words were from the Lord. *"All of a sudden, everyone gathers together. With an opponent on the other side, everyone **becomes one – they become a team**. That is what today's luncheon is about. Today, it's time for the whistle to be blown. It is time for us to gather together – from different places and different "positions" because the game is getting ready to start."*

The presence of the Lord was so strong in that room. I could see the heads of the pastors nodding in agreement as this message of calling together the Church was coming forth. I started to try to say a few words about Reggie and his resume. After a sentence or two, Reggie stood up and cut me off, "Don't worry about it," he said as he grabbed the microphone and began to speak. Twenty-four years later, I couldn't even tell you what he talked about. I can tell you that what happened that day changed my life. God was laying the groundwork for unity within his Church and he was doing so in a powerful way.

By the end of the luncheon that day, all sixty churches represented had signed on to the event. I genuinely believe that what God was about to do in our city would not have happened had this foundation of unity not been in place. In Psalm 133, the unity of God's people is connected to God's blessing. <u>His blessing flows from His people united</u> and the city of Madison was about to experience what that meant.

We rented the Dane County Coliseum (known today as the Alliant Energy Center) in the heart of Madison, WI. The crusade spanned over four nights, and each night seemed to build upon the one before. Each session was significant, but I will never forget the final night. Our focus was on young people that night. We had a great band, Audio Adrenaline, performing, and things were supposed to kick off at 7pm. Around 6:50 pm, I could see people were still pouring in the doors. I ran up to the top deck of the coliseum and looked out over Madison's main highway. Traffic was backed up as cars were trying to exit and make their way to the coliseum parking lot! It was amazing. We pushed back the start time to allow everyone trying to get in ample time. Lowell Lundstrom spoke and then gave an invitation for the crowd to respond. At that moment, it was like the Lord swung a sickle across that auditorium. People from all over the arena got up out of their seats and made their way to the front to receive Christ. That week in Madison, Wisconsin – a place some have referred to as a spiritual graveyard – 1,479 people gave their lives to Christ. My heart exploded with joy as I tried to take in what was happening. So many people had chosen to put their faith in Jesus. It was an incredible honor to witness.

As things were wrapping up that final night, we sat – kind of in a daze soaking up what had just taken place. Lowell put his arm around my neck and gave me his rough, cowboy version of a hug. He said, "Son, that was a miracle of God. In forty years of ministry, I've never seen anything like that happen."

This event was never about one ministry, one person, or one church being honored in the spotlight. It truly was, from beginning to end, about the renown of the name of Jesus Christ. And what Jesus did was off the charts. The body of Christ was unified. The Son of God was glorified. Lives were changed for eternity.

The many different pastors involved with the crusade on stage with evangelist Lowell Lundstrom. Madison, WI.

The reason I share this story with you is twofold. Firstly, my aim is simply to honor the Lord and what he did. I like to tell the details of this story because **only God** could orchestrate things this incredibly. Secondly, I want to encourage you with an example of how God used a regular business guy to do something supernatural. *Please*, don't disqualify yourself because you don't have a certain title or level of experience. *Never* think God can't or doesn't want to use you to be part of bringing those who don't yet know him into His Kingdom. You have been created for good works that the Lord has prepared in advance for you to do. Your responsibility is to be obedient. In doing so, your life will impact the lives of more people than you can imagine.

Here's one more stunning piece to the story. The following year the unity of the body of Christ was on display again. We worked together to organize a crusade focused on the youth in our area – "The Edge 2000." Thousands of young people gave their lives to Jesus and committed to follow him. Even better, they were plugged into youth groups in the area. We are still feeling the ripple effects of this event in our city today.

CHAPTER 4

Bryan Peterson

2000. Madison, WI.

Here's the thing, I'm a businessman – and many of my friends are pastors – **But that doesn't mean that pastors and businesspeople can't work together.** I'm telling you what – the Lord has something in the works right now, preparing for marketplace people and pastors to function **together**.

You just read two stories where there was really an unprecedented level of unity on display amongst the body of Christ in our city. There were so many amazing things that came out of the relationships built during both the Elizabeth House as well as the crusade. While there is no time to share them all, here is one I think you'll find particularly encouraging.

My friend, Bryan Peterson, has been a Pastor in Madison for 31 years, and I'd like him to share this story with you. The church he pastors was started in 1949 by his grandfather, Norman Peterson Sr., and continues to impact the city of Madison to this day…

Pastor Bryan: "East Washington Avenue is the main artery into the heart of downtown Madison, WI. Our church was a little square building that had been constructed in 1956 and sat right on East Wash. This story takes place in the late 90s and we were in desperate need of a modest expansion to accommodate our ministry growth.

Over the years, we had acquired a couple of houses next to the church – so the idea of expansion wasn't outside the realm of possibility. There was a city ordinance in place that required buildings over 10,000 sq/ft to go through the city planning commission and the neighborhood association before expansion could occur. This ordinance served as a protection for local neighborhoods to prevent significant commercial buildings from coming in and destroying a neighborhood, but it also meant we had to jump through a few hoops before proceeding.

Our proposal was modest – we only needed to move one of the houses our church had already acquired. Better yet, no residents needed to be relocated. We took our crude drawing of the expansion down to the next city planning commission meeting. We learned there that a small group of neighbors didn't want to see the expansion take place. Because of the opposition from those two or three neighbors, the planning commission slammed the door on us.

Throughout this process, we learned that the alderman for our neighborhood was siding with the few people who weren't interested in having us there. My family and I lived in this neighborhood – one block from the church – so this guy was not just the alderman representing our church, but my family and I as well. I continued to reach out but felt like my words fell on deaf ears. Our alderman was very resistant and I felt we had nowhere to go.

I explained to our elders at church that we were probably done with this idea of expansion. If we wanted to grow, we'd have to go elsewhere. We tabled the idea of expansion in our current location and began to pray about what the Lord would have us do next. During this time, we had our building appraised and were actively looking into relocation options.

A couple of years went by, and through the crusade story you just read about, I met Dave and we began a friendship. One afternoon, we were out to lunch with Dave and Jean and another couple on the West side of Madison. Dave doesn't do anything small, so instead of meeting him at the restaurant, he picked us all up in his 35ft. RV. After we ate, we drove up on some land owned by the archdiocese of Madison. Dave said it was a piece of land he was considering purchasing to build a new health club, so he asked if we'd join with him in prayer. We did, and as we wrapped up, Dave mentioned the name of our alderman. It was kind of out of the blue and I was surprised to find out Dave knew him. "I know I'm supposed to love like Jesus, but I have to be honest – I don't like that guy very much," I said to Dave. I was being brutally honest as the interactions I had with that alderman had kind of left a bitter taste in my mouth.

Turns out Dave had built a relationship with this man through previous dealings and had even been praying for and sharing Christ with him. He said to me, "If you ever need me to meet with you and this alderman, give me a call. I would love to just be a voice and somebody to support you in this effort."

I told him I appreciated him saying that and that I'd keep it in mind. But I really had no desire to meet with or talk to this alderman again. I wanted to just relocate.

The Spring of 2000 rolled around and we were still looking into relocation options since expanding our current building wasn't an option. During this time, the city of Madison had begun a master plan to beautify the neighborhoods along East Washington Avenue. They were working with four or five different neighborhood associations when the president of our neighborhood association came to us and said, "We don't want your church to leave our neighborhood." It was a nice thing to hear, but my eyes were still set on a new location.

Dave Gerry

Following the news from our neighborhood president, I got a call from the head of the planning commission for the city of Madison. He told me we had his recommendation that our church stayed and asked if there was anything he could do to help ensure we didn't relocate. I was baffled as this was the same guy who, three years earlier had completely opposed us when we presented our idea of expanding.

I could tell God was moving, but it felt like a mountain was in our way. Even though things seemed to be shifting in our favor, we still needed approval from our neighborhood association – which meant we still needed to meet with our alderman. You have to understand a few years earlier we had been rejected so severely, it was embarrassing. Our alderman wouldn't take my calls and the thought of trying to reach out again was intimidating.

I finally got up the guts to call him, but he didn't have time to talk. The frustration of our past dealings began to bubble up inside of me. But I remembered the things the Lord was putting into place, so I pressed in. I left another message explaining that we had the recommendation from the head of the planning commission. Upon hearing this, he agreed to meet with us. I immediately called Dave and shared that we had managed to schedule a meeting with the alderman and asked if he would join us in the meeting. Dave agreed and I'll never forget what happened next.

I showed up to the meeting the following week along with a couple of our elders. As we were walking in from the parking lot, Dave pulled in. He jumped out of his car and proceeded to open the door for all of us. A few minutes later, the alderman came in. We greeted one another and he looked right at Dave, "Oh, Mr. Gerry, I didn't know that you went to church here."

Dave said, "Well, I don't… but my brother and his family do, as well as my parents. Bryan is a friend of mine and he asked me to join you all today."

It's hard to explain, but in that moment, it was like the alderman became a member of our team. He instantly became a friend – which he had never been before. In the office that day, he basically told us, "Whatever you need, I'm your man." He did a 180 on the spot. I could hardly believe my ears.

We had three more public meetings with the neighbors and the neighborhood association and the favor we were shown was tremendous. Our neighborhood president had gotten seventy signatures from neighbors on a petition for our church to stay!

Things were leaning in our direction, but this process wasn't over. We still needed our petition to pass through the planning commission – and there was still one neighbor standing in direct opposition to us.

Monday, September 10, 2001, we gathered in downtown Madison for a final planning commission meeting. I had the opportunity to speak and present our case to the commission. As that time drew near, my nerves increased. I remember looking out across the room as the meeting was about to begin and seeing Dave come flying in. He made his way toward the board of commissioners and sat down right next to our neighborhood's alderman. I could see they were talking and tried not to let doubt creep in. A few minutes later, just as the meeting was beginning, Dave got up and made his way to the door. I caught his eye and he gave me a thumbs-up as he walked out. It was the funniest thing, but a wave of relief swept over me. "We've got this," I thought to myself. It was like the Lord was giving me the encouragement I needed in what had been a very challenging and emotional process. That evening, our petition – not only to stay, but to expand – was passed. **Unanimously**. God called our church to be an outpost for this part of the city and it was His plan for us to stay. Little did we know how desperately our city would need support in the midst of the chaos that would envelop the country the next day.

Over the last two decades, that addition has been used daily for families with preschool children, weekly for our children, youth & adult ministries, and monthly for our mobile food pantry and neighborhood association meetings. The gym has provided space for wedding & funeral receptions, basketball nights for neighborhood kids, and Harvest Festival celebrations where we have welcomed as many as 700 parents and children from our community for an evening of games, candy, food, and fun. It has been a tremendous blessing not only to our congregation but to the surrounding community as well.

The Lord could have chosen many different ways to accomplish his purpose of our church staying in that community. But in this instance, he used my friend Dave to open the door for us. Here's the thing: I can't gain entrance into the places that Dave operates in because my gifts and talents don't function in that arena. Just like Dave's gifts and talents don't function in the role of a pastor. **For me to go out and try to take on the calling and leading that the Lord has in Dave's life would be the biggest waste of time. I'm not even wired to do that. I'm not called to do that.** That's why we need each other. We need to stay in our lanes and remember that we are in this together. The Lord uses each of us in the body of Christ to strengthen his purpose and his Kingdom plan.

Like Dave said at the opening of this chapter: Why can't pastors and business people work together? **They can.** And this story illustrates what that can look like. As each of us operates in our giftings and callings, there is no limit to what the Lord can accomplish through our lives. Unity matters to God and it will take all of us in the body of Christ for His plan and purpose to be fulfilled on earth.

CHAPTER 5

Mike Kuglitsch

2006. New Berlin, WI.

As the Princeton Club continued to grow in Madison, we set our sights on the Milwaukee market. With a population of nearly 600,000 residents, Milwaukee was an exciting new frontier for us as a company. We began looking for available pieces of land or existing health club locations.

In the process, we connected with Mike Kuglitsch and his business partner. Mike's business partner was a former Princeton Club member and together they now owned a health club in the Milwaukee suburb of New Berlin. It was called Motion Fitness and Racquet Club and when they heard that we wanted to expand into that territory, Mike's business partner reached out. His contact was my brother, Ted – the manager at the East Side Princeton Club. Ted had developed an informal advisory relationship with this man during his tenure as a member of our club, and they had several conversations about the health club industry prior to Motion being built. As a builder and developer with a lifelong interest in fitness, he proceeded to build a very nice health club in New Berlin. He teamed up with Mike and a couple of other guys to create Motion Fitness.

After being in operation for five years, they heard The Princeton Club was looking to come into that area. They weren't interested in competing with us and instead wanted to pursue the idea of having The Princeton Club buy them out. As I toured their 146,000 sq/ft facility for the first time, it was obvious it had been built around the model of the Princeton Club. They had a large cardio deck, strength training area, basketball courts, a lap pool, indoor/outdoor tennis courts, a cycling studio, a childcare facility, and much more. They had taken a page right out of our book! They had built it just like I would have. All of this made the idea of acquiring Motion Fitness even more lucrative. Instead of finding land and building a new Princeton Club from scratch, we could purchase this existing club and inherit its 6,000 members. This would allow us to transition ownership without ever closing the club for business.

The next step was to determine whether the Princeton Club would keep the existing 75 employees on staff at Motion Fitness or replace them with new hires. As with any business, lining up the right staff is crucial – especially for a smooth transition. In order for us to make that decision, we needed to get to know the existing general manager, Mike Kuglistch.

Mike had run the club since its inception in 2002. It was nearing the end of November 2006 and we hoped to finalize the deal before the new year. While Mike had had several meetings with our CFO, Scott and our West Side Club Manager, Pete – he and I had yet to sit down and get to know one another. I'll let him tell the story from here:

Mike: As conversations about the purchase of Motion Fitness were taking place, I had several meetings with some of the executive team from the Princeton Club. Despite these interactions, we never had any finalization of what my role would look like once the sale was complete. The end of the year was drawing near, so I called Dave and said, "Hey, we should really talk about this."

He said, "Why don't Pete and I come down to Milwaukee and we'll have a conversation."

My understanding was that this was going to be an interview. I told my wife about this meeting, and I was sure I'd leave having an answer for her as to whether or not I had a job going forward.

I was glad to be sitting down with these guys to get some answers. We met in a conference room off-site, away from the club. "I assume this is an interview and we can kind of figure out where we're going to go from here..." I said, hoping Dave or Pete would jump in with some clarity.

Dave said, "Well, that was the plan, but as we were driving down today, I really felt like instead of a formal interview, we should just sit down and talk – you know, get to know each other."

"Ok," I said. "Talk about what?"

He went on, "Who are the people who have had the most impact on your life?"

I could tell this wasn't going to be a traditional job interview. "Well, my father would be the first – I've learned so much from him about character and business. And then second would be my college wrestling coach."

"Why?" asked Dave.

"Our team was pretty young – and a little bit crazy," I said. "But my coach really kept us in line. He helped get the best out of us in competition, but also kept us focused on what really mattered – getting our degrees and seeing the bigger picture in life. He was a born-again Christian, so he helped keep us morally grounded."

I remember when I said, "born again" it was like Dave's radar went up. He goes, "So, born again Christian – do you know what that is?"

I said, "Not really." I had grown up in the Catholic church but didn't have an answer. Dave took a few minutes to explain what that term meant. He laid out the gospel in a very simple and real way… and then we **really just started a conversation** about it. We talked about faith and life. I told him how I had conversations about this stuff with a friend of mine in the past, but that I was always left wondering.

"You know, I said, 'I've always kind of walked around the pool and put my toe in, but I've never really decided to jump in.'"

"Why is that?" asked Dave.

We talked about some of the various reasons why and then I remember saying, "I've kind of been ready for years, but **I just don't know how to do it.**"

Dave told me he sensed I was ready to make that move. "When I was at that point in my life,' he said, 'someone helped lead me in a prayer – is that something you'd like to do today?'"

I said, "Dave, I'm ready."

As we began to pray together, I suddenly felt this huge weight come off me. It was like I was being overtaken and was experiencing a sense of lightness – a real sense of peace. Almost 17 years later, I still get emotional whenever I tell this part of the story.

We went on to talk for another hour just about the Lord and what our main purpose on earth is. But then the meeting just kind of ended. It's funny looking back now, but we never even talked about the job. I drove home feeling so full. That's really the best way I can describe it: my heart was just full. I realized that I had spent my life chasing things that don't last – like money and fame – individual stuff. And what happened that day was eternal. I had finally said, "Ok God, I surrender." And the peace I had is hard to describe.

I got home and my wife said, "How did the interview go?... Are you going to have a job when this all happens?"

I said, "I don't know."

I laugh about this conversation now, but in the moment, it was all a bit confusing. She said, "What do you mean?"

"Well, we never actually talked about the job. We ended up talking about God and faith and what's important in life."

My wife is in HR, so she said, "You can't talk about that in an interview."

"Well, we did… and you know, I'm okay with it."

She was as baffled as I was. Neither one of us knew if I was going to have a job in a month… yet for some reason it seemed like it was all going to work out. I waited a couple of days and then followed up with Dave again. "The other day was great and I appreciate it. But when I got home my wife asked if I got the job, and I didn't know what to tell her…"

He said, "You know what, don't worry about it. Everything will be fine."

He still never said I had a job. "Let me just work a few things out and then we'll talk soon."

Literally, a week or two before the final sale took place, I received a call from Dave. "Hey Mike, I've been praying about it and I want you to continue running the club down there as a GM. There's an individual that I first had pegged for that position, but I think he would really grow under your mentorship."

I said, "Ok, great. What about compensation?"

"I'll have Scott call you and you guys can work that out."

I trusted that Dave and the Princeton Club would do the right thing for me and my family. And it has worked out. My faith has grown, and my wife's faith has grown – we have been going to a non-denominational Christian church pretty much since then. And I've told Dave this: "I'm a better father, I'm a better husband, I'm just a better individual since I accepted the Lord, and if it wasn't for that day, I think I'd still be walking around the pool putting my toe in and not jumping in…for that, I will thank you for the rest of my life."

When you get close to the inner circle within the Princeton Club organization, you realize it's about more than fitness and making money. Those are important, but it's about helping people find the Lord, and we do that through the fellowship of the organization. I have benefitted, my family has benefitted, and I'll be forever grateful to Dave for that time. I've learned through this journey that the Lord puts people in positions, and at that point in my life, the Lord put Dave and the Princeton Club in front of me to change my life. I'm simply grateful.

Dave: Mike's story is so genuine and real. I've listened to him share this story with various groups of people over the years, and each time, tears have welled up in my eyes. Here's something you need to know though: going into that meeting, I didn't have an agenda to lead him to Jesus. I was not trying to force or manipulate the situation. My plan was to interview him and see if he'd be a good fit as a general manager for the Princeton Club. That was it. However, I *did* go in sensitive to the Holy Spirit and to what He wanted to do that day. In this instance, as I drove to meet Mike, I just knew in my spirit: *This guy is going to accept Christ today.* It's hard to explain, but I had that sense – somewhere between my chest and belly button – that the Lord had a more significant plan than just a job interview that day. That is why I pressed into a Gospel-centered conversation. Never forget: The Holy Spirit is the one who leads, and the Holy Spirit is the one who transforms hearts. Not us.

CHAPTER 6

Whose Kingdom?

2000. Madison, WI.

It's almost time for you to set this book down and live out your own stories. But before you do, I need to introduce you to another friend, Chris Conrad. Chris and I met 23 years ago and I think you'll enjoy him starting this one off...

Chris: My wife Mary and I had just moved to Madison. After planting and pastoring a thriving church in South Dakota, we sensed Holy Spirit calling us to Wisconsin.

I had been in Madison for a few weeks before a friend told me I should consider connecting with a guy named Dave Gerry. I began to seek him out. He's not an easy man to get ahold of, but after leaving several messages for him at his work, he finally called me back. I explained that I was a new pastor in town and was hoping to get together with him. He agreed and we scheduled a meeting at the East Side Princeton Club.

Now, I was a church planter and I needed to raise money. I'm not proud to admit this, but it's true – it didn't take me long to figure out Dave had financial resources. Upon arriving at the Health

Club, he asked if I'd like to walk across the street with him to grab a bite to eat at Culver's. In the short walk, I gave him my best sales pitch. I was trying to convince him that I was worth whatever check he wanted to write. It's embarrassing for me to think about now, but my pitch was shameless.

Dave: Chris seemed nervous as we sat down to have our lunch. He was talking non-stop. This gave me enough time to finish my burger, so I didn't mind. He was really trying to pitch me an idea I could invest in. He was really selling his vision and product. He was a church planter and he needed help.

As I sat there listening to Chris share his heart, the Holy Spirit prompted me to ask him a question. It was not an easy question and was made especially difficult considering I had just met the man. When Chris paused to take a bite of his burger (his first bite, by the way) I said, "I have a question to ask you… but if I do, I may never see you again." He set his burger down and straightened up, anticipating what I was about to say. I think the Lord wants me to ask you: **"Whose Kingdom did you come here to build, yours or God's?"**

Chris: When Dave asked me that question, it cut me to the heart. I immediately began to cry – while sitting at Culver's with a cheeseburger in front of me. It was a bit embarrassing. But what was happening was this: Dave, under the inspiration of the Holy Spirit, had just called me up short. He asked me the question that needed to be asked, and the Lord used it to cut through my arrogance and insecurity.

Dave: I wasn't sure what was happening, but I knew right from that moment that God's hand was on this guy. It was so evident the Lord was doing something in him. I suggested we head back to my office, so he could have some privacy. While on the walk over to the health club, I shared with Chris three specific things about the Kingdom of God. As we walked through the front doors of the health club, I brought him right into my brother Ted's office. Ted has managed the East Side club for 30 years and loves the Lord. He had no idea Chris and I were coming in. He was just working hard, doing his stuff. His door was open, so I poked my head in and said, "Hey Ted, are you free?"

He said he was, so I quickly introduced the two. I said, "Ted, this is Pastor Chris... Chris, this is my brother Ted. Ted, would you pray for Chris?"

"Yeah, I'd be happy to," said Ted. He motioned for Chris to have a seat in the chair across the desk from him. As Chris sat down, I headed for the door.

I thanked Ted, and turned to Chris, "Hey, it's been great meeting you. I'll talk to you later."

And I left.

Now, Ted's version of the story includes me pushing Chris in the door, shutting it behind him, and leaving – awkwardly interrupting Ted in his work. We'll let you be the judge of that. The point is there were no words spoken about what had just happened at Culvers, nor what Chris and I discussed walking back over.

Chris: Dave just left. And there I was with this guy, his brother, whom I had just met 10 seconds ago. *This is not how I thought this was going to go*, I thought to myself as I sat there waiting for Ted to pray. My eyes were still puffy from my encounter with the Holy Spirit. Little did I know, the Lord wasn't finished with me yet. It was a very interesting experience. I came with hopes of raising funds for my church plant, but the Lord had a different idea. Ted has an incredible prophetic gift and I was about to find that out. He began to pray, and over the next few moments, he prayed for me the *exact three things* that Dave had just spoken to me on our walk back from Culvers.

As Ted began to pray, the first thing he said was, "Whose Kingdom are you building?"

I was shocked. He just prayed the exact question that Dave had asked me at Culvers. That got my attention. Ted proceeded to lay his hand on my shoulder and what happened next is hard to describe. The following 15 minutes were absolutely life changing. The power of God touched me and I fell out of my chair, hitting the wall behind me. Ted continued to pray that I would be set free and filled with the Holy Spirit. I began to speak in other tongues as I was baptized in the Holy Spirit. God was doing such a deep work inside of me. It was one of the most radical encounters I had ever had in the presence of the Lord.

When it came time to say goodbye to Ted, Dave was nowhere to be found. Turns out he had not only left the office, but the entire building. As I drove home later that afternoon, I called Dave. I just *had* to know if he had told Ted anything about our conversation over lunch. The things Ted prayed were so specific and he repeated some of the exact same points… but Dave reassured me he hadn't.

As I reflect on this experience, it is God's power through marketplace people that strikes me the most. If you are a marketplace person, please do not ever think to yourself that you cannot make a powerful impact on those who get their paychecks from a church. One of the most profound moments of my life took place… not in a church… but in the marketplace. Remember when Dave's pastor prayed over him and God moved him to chair the crusade? The wonderful truth of the Kingdom is that it *goes both ways*. When we are operating fully in our gifts, those with a marketplace anointing can have a powerful impact on pastors just as pastors can have an impact on those with a marketplace anointing.

Dave: We are all building the Kingdom of God – one beautiful, obedient step at a time. We are part of an interconnected body and are designed to support one another. Sometimes, as we are following the promptings of the Holy Spirit, this might look like a role reversal. Like in this story… a couple of business guys ministering to a pastor. But if your daily approach truly is to remain sensitive to the Holy Spirit and what He wants to do… then obey… the Lord may invite you into things that are outside the traditional box you have in your mind. It's such a blast, and you know what? It's really that simple. Not always *easy*, but simple.

CHAPTER 7

Identity

2016. Scottsdale, AZ.

"You are not God's employees – you are his sons." The group of nine pastors sitting in my living room were staring back at me as I spoke these words. These guys were seasoned ministers – each having congregations of 1,000 or more. They had been Christ followers for much of their lives, but there was something about those words that hit them in a new way that afternoon. The Holy Spirit was doing a work in their hearts, stripping away the performance identity they had slipped back into.

Have you ever found yourself in that place? Maybe you started off well intentioned, but somewhere along the journey, your walk with God moved from relational to transactional. If what you do *for* God has somehow become more important than simply walking *with God*, this chapter is for you.

A few months before this group of pastors were sitting in my living room, Chris Conrad had reached out to me. This is the same Chris Conrad from the story you just read in the last chapter, though 16 years of friendship had taken place in between. He asked if he could bring a group of pastors to my home for a retreat. Chris had been promoted to district superintendent and was responsible for overseeing over 160 Wesleyan churches in the Midwest. A big part of his job is to serve, encourage, and empower church leaders to be successful. His desire is to resource those on the front lines with what they need to raise the next generation to advance the Kingdom of God. One of the ways he serves these leaders is by occasionally taking a small group of them on a two- or three-day retreat. The goal is to create a space for them to be together, away from their everyday routine. He wants them to have fun, rest, and seek the Lord and what He is saying to them.

Chris and I team up really well together, so I want to tell the rest of this story with him...

Chris: Dave agreed to host us and we decided on a date three months out. Here's the funny part: Dave and Jean live in Wisconsin, but they also have a winter home in Arizona. Our retreat was going to be in March, and Dave was under the impression that the pastors and I would use their home in Wisconsin while they were out of town. It wasn't until I checked in with Dave to share our flight information **two days prior to our arrival** that he realized we were coming to stay with them in Arizona.

Dave: The funniest part of this story is that when I got off the phone with Chris, I had to go explain the miscommunication to my wife. I told Jean that the group of nine pastors were not heading to Wisconsin, but to Arizona. And we'd be hosting them. After the initial shock wore off, Jean switched into "hospitality-mode" and prepared our home to receive and feed this group of men. She was incredible. She is so gifted at serving and making others feel safe and welcome in our home.

Chris: I couldn't believe how Dave and I had miscommunicated, but the way that he, Jean and their daughter, Jessie, served us those few days was phenomenal. They hosted us like kings. They set the table, both literally and figuratively, for the Holy Spirit to do what he wanted to do in the lives of these pastors.

Dave: After scrambling a bit to get things ready, Chris and the pastors arrived. I invited them to make themselves at home. My plan was to just disappear and let them have free reign to do their thing. It was a typical sunny Arizona afternoon, so the crew headed to the backyard to sit outside around the fire pit for their initial "meeting." Chris pulled me aside and asked if I was ready to share – to which I replied, *"Uh, I'm sorry, what?"*

Chris: Dave and I are much more in sync now, but for some reason our communication was clearly not firing on all cylinders during that first retreat. I had brought this group to hang out *with* Dave – and Dave thought he was supposed to give us space and leave us alone. Well, actually Dave thought we were going to Wisconsin. We laugh a lot about it now.

Dave: I didn't want to disappoint Chris, but I had nothing prepared to share with these pastors. I remember walking outside and sitting down with them. Everyone was in a circle around the fire. I thought, *"Lord, help me. What do you want me to say to these guys?"*

Chris: I introduced Dave to the group and shared a little bit about his business background with them. Then Dave proceeded to say something I was definitely not expecting. He looked around the circle and said, *"You know, to be honest with you guys, I really don't care that much about your ministries..."* You could have heard a pin drop. Thankfully, he continued, *"...but I deeply, deeply care about you as men."*

That was the first time in years that some of these pastors had heard someone say something like that to them. Everyone wanted a part of them… for some reason. People wanted to meet with them to help them with their marriages. People wanted to meet with them to help with some addiction or area in their life that wasn't right. Pastors of smaller churches wanted to meet with them to figure out their "secret sauce" of why their churches were growing. In short, everyone wanted something FROM them. Not only that, but leading a large church can become who you are. For many, their jobs become their identity. If you gain any level of notoriety, you can easily become a persona.

It had been years since someone looked these pastors in the eye and said, "I don't care about the size of your church… I care about YOU." In other words, I want more FOR you than I want FROM you. In that moment, the presence of God settled over all of us. It was tangible. Dave began to weep, not in an emotional way, but in intercession. He's really not an emotional guy, but when he encounters the presence of God, he is undone.

Dave: I remember when those words came out of my mouth, I experienced thirty seconds or so of intense intercession in my spirit. This doesn't happen to me all the time, but when it does, it is a powerful experience with the Holy Spirit. It's like the Lord was validating the words that were just spoken. When I lifted my head up, I'm telling you, I could've said anything I wanted at that point and those men would have listened. It was like God used that line to unlock something deep in their hearts in preparation for what he wanted to do.

Over the next thirty-six hours, the Lord ministered powerfully to this group of pastors. Chris and I, a pastor and a businessman – *together* – followed the lead of the Holy Spirit. It was a blast. We had many impromptu times of telling stories about what God had done in each of our lives (some of the same stories you've read in this book!) As I wrapped up one of those times, I paused and said that line from the beginning of this chapter: *"**You are not God's employees. You are his sons.**"* I remember watching that reality sink in. Collectively, it was like the weight of performance was coming off of them. They even relaxed physically – reclining back in their chairs and on the couch. It was really cool. I encouraged them to quit worrying about all the expectations placed on them – both from other people and from themselves. They were beginning to rest in the truth that they were favored sons of the Most High King. What an amazing reality!

As we transitioned from this time into our next meal together, one of the pastors pulled me aside. He told me, "You said something a little bit ago that changed my life. I've never seen myself as a son of God. I've *always* seen myself as his employee. I will never be the same after hearing that sentence."

How about you? Have you seen yourself more as God's employee than his child? Are you striving to perform and earn his acceptance – even though you already have it? Because the truth is this: There is nothing you could ever do that would change the love your Father in heaven has for you. Nothing. He loves you, because he loves you.

The difference between an employee and a son or daughter is huge. Take my own son, Teddy, for example. He's now a full-grown man, 31 years old, with a wife and three children. I'm so proud of him and the man he has grown to be. He is brilliant, hardworking, inventive, and funny. My love for him is so deep, and there is nothing he has ever done or could do that will change that.

When he was a boy, not even tall enough to see over the front desk, he would come to visit me in the health club. We have free child care at the Princeton Club for members to utilize while they workout, so my kids always enjoyed coming to play there when they had the opportunity. In addition to spending some time in the playroom with his friends, Teddy would occasionally want to explore other areas of the health club. We don't allow kids under the age of twelve on the workout floor for safety purposes, but when he was with me, he could go anywhere. I would take him around and show him all the equipment. He was such a cute little guy and would quickly make friends with bodybuilder men – giants compared to him. Sometimes I would let him try a piece of equipment out – he'd hop on the treadmill, and I'd push the button to turn it on. He was a speedy kid on the soccer field, so this was one of his favorites.

Even if I wasn't with him, he was able to go to the front desk and politely ask the receptionist to do something that they wouldn't do for any other child. He would ask for a basketball to go shoot hoops in the gym or for a racquet to go play racquetball with his sister. He could even ask them to lower the volleyball nets in the gym if he wanted to play, and they would oblige. I taught him that he was allowed to do this, though always with respect and manners. But here's the thing, this little kid, because he was my son, had *access* to people and places in my health club that no other child had. And this is why: before he ever went to an employee to ask for something, he had to first come into my office. He had access to me whenever he wanted, and he had to ask my permission to do something before he did it. Once I granted him permission to go use the gymnasium, he then could go to the front desk and ask an employee for help. As the owner, I have authority to make decisions about how we are going to carry out our business. I can invite whomever I like into the club, and it is up to my discretion how I choose to delegate my authority. As my son, he had authority in the health club on a level other children, members and even employees did not.

One more thing. As my son, Teddy's relationship with me has nothing to do with what he has done. While the employees that work for me receive payment based on their performance, my son receives an inheritance just because he is my son. An employee can be fired for making a mistake. My son will *never* not be my son. An employee has limited access to me – usually just at work. My son has full access to me – any time, any place.

This is exactly how it is with your heavenly Father and his kingdom. As a child of God, you have access to your Father in a unique and special way. A way in which those who are not his children may not approach him. I love how the writer of Hebrews speaks of this access: "Let us then approach God's throne of grace with confidence, so that we may receive mercy and find grace to help us in our time of need."[4] If you have surrendered your life to the Lordship of Jesus and have been born again as his child, you have been chosen, redeemed, purposed, predestined, marked, and given an inheritance in His Kingdom. Your Father in heaven longs to have a relationship with you… not as his employee, but as his child. So just like the pastors in my living room were reminded of who they are as sons of God, allow the truth of the Word of God to remind you of your position in the family of Christ:

You are loved. You are redeemed. You are precious. You are powerful. You are beautiful. You are chosen. You are important. You are forgiven. You are a new creation. You are predestined. You are a royal priesthood. You are an heir of God and co-heir with Christ. You are lovely. You are not alone. You are fearfully and wonderfully made. You are favored. You have been saved and called to a holy life. You have been empowered and given authority. You have purpose.

You are a child of God. You are HIS.

---

[4] Hebrews 4:16 NIV

CHAPTER 8

Interns

Every summer for five years, I had 3 recent high school graduates intern with me. It was a 40-hour-per-week paid internship that lasted the entire summer. I simply invited them to come along for everything I did in a day. The only requirement was: keep up... and I like to move fast. This meant board meetings and bank meetings. It meant learning commercial real estate and health club operations. It even meant tough manual labor as needs arose. I wanted them to be my shadow, and I desired to open doors for them to get into environments they wouldn't normally be in at their age. More than that, I wanted them to understand in their heart that they could love and serve God while working in the marketplace. I wanted them to know they could serve in their local church, live in submission to their pastoral leadership, lead and love their families AND be successful business people.

My wife, Jean, usually seemed to know who the interns were supposed to be before I did. It was like the Lord would reveal it to her so she could begin praying for them. Then, at some point along the way, the Lord would make it clear to me too. It mattered a great deal that we were unified on this because these kids became a big part of our lives in that season. They spent a lot of time with me, which meant a lot of time with my family. Looking back, I am so appreciative for how each intern was a solid role model for my kids to be around.

It was during this season the Lord began teaching me about the life of David in the Bible. It became clear that this message was what the Holy Spirit wanted me to teach the interns. David's life was the first biblical account of one person operating in three different anointings: prophet, priest, and king. *Anointing* is the empowerment of God to function powerfully, skillfully, and effectively in a specific setting or sphere of influence. It's something that is outside of your natural ability to do on your own. An anointing isn't a spiritual gift, but the two are closely related. So, David functioned in this "triune anointing" of prophet, priest, and king. In this way, his life was a Messianic foreshadowing of Jesus. He was clearly imperfect, yet he was the first person God gifted to function in all three areas very seamlessly.

Most of the interns I had, and many of you reading this book, have this triune anointing as well. You have an anointing from God to function in prophetic, priestly, and kingly ways. All three. How? Let's look at each one.

Prophetic Anointing

We are told by the Apostle Paul to earnestly desire to prophesy. Prophecy is a gift God has given to his Church. It is a sign for believers[5] and an incredible means by which to upbuild, encourage and console people.[6] It is never intended to replace Scripture, but it is a powerful gift that brings so much life to believers. Functioning in this anointing might look like praying for someone and, by the power of the Holy Spirit, knowing what the Lord is saying to that

---

[5] 1 Corinthians 14:22

[6] 1 Corinthians 14:3

person. It might look like having an understanding of things God is calling to be done in the future. Or it might be sharing a word with someone so specific to the secrets in their heart, it leads them to repentance, or to knowing more deeply how God intimately loves them. I've seen this prophetic anointing in action time and time again, and having it released and active amongst believers brings such strength, encouragement, and hope.

Priestly Anointing

In the Old Testament, priests were the ones designated by God to minister before the Lord in the inner sanctuary of the tabernacle. In the New Testament, all believers are a part of a royal priesthood. 1 Peter 2:9 says, "But you are a chosen people, a royal priesthood, a holy nation, God's special possession, that you may declare the praises of him who called you out of darkness into his wonderful light." In some capacity, every believer today can function in a priestly role. I don't mean that every believer is called to be a pastor or priest in a vocational sense, but every believer is called to have a private life of devotion before the Lord. We are created to worship, pray, and study the Word of God. This all falls under a priestly anointing. This was modeled in the life of David in many ways. He was a worshiper. He was a man of prayer. He was a man of the Word.

Most often today, we see this anointing on display inside the local church. Pastors, priests, and worship leaders all function in this anointing. But it doesn't stop there. This priestly anointing also means caring for a friend in need, counseling a neighbor through a difficult season, or sharing the Gospel with that coworker you always run into at lunch. Simply stopping to pray with someone the Lord puts on your heart is an example of leading another into the presence of God.

Kingly Anointing

The term 'kingly' does not mean sitting on a throne with a scepter and telling people what to do. That is how we see it on display in the Bible as there were literal kings anointed by prophets to lead people. Today, we can think of it as a person who is gifted in business, education, government, entertainment, military, or economics (or some combination of all these areas). They are often leaders, entrepreneurial, and apostolic in their nature. This anointing is designed to help advance the Kingdom of God across the earth both inside AND outside the local church. It is most powerfully on display when the one carrying it functions with the heart of a servant in humility, generosity, and the fear of the Lord.

*****

Back to the interns. These young people were sharp. They were smart, ambitious, talented, and they truly loved the Lord. It was clear they wanted to serve him with their lives, but like many people their age, they were working out what that looked like. As I walked with them during this season, it was obvious they were wrestling with which "one-third" of their anointing they were supposed to choose to function in for the rest of their lives. Can you imagine? Living your life one-third alive because you didn't know that each anointing was not mutually exclusive? What a tragedy.

My job as their mentor was to teach them it doesn't have to be that way. I wanted to help model what it looked like to function in all three. Remember the story I told at the beginning of this book about the auditorium full of CEOs and the line from Henry Blackaby that made us squirm in our seats? "If you were really holy, you would quit your jobs and become missionaries in Africa."

His point was not that there is anything wrong with being a missionary in Africa. We *absolutely* need missionaries sharing the gospel with unreached people groups across the earth. The point was that it would be wrong for us to think if we really wanted to love and serve God that we *only have one option*. **Our God is so much bigger than that.** He intentionally created each of us with unique giftings and passions. It's actually by His perfect design that we aren't all called to the exact same thing.

Hear me in this: If you were *really* holy, you would do *exactly* what Jesus Christ died for you to do. Nothing more. Nothing less. Earnestly seeking and simply obeying. Functioning *exactly* where He's placed you to function. And do you know what? When you do so, there will be grace, simplicity, and freedom in your life to run the race that God has uniquely designed you to run. Your passions and giftings will align and you will experience such purpose in everything you do.

Here's a great example. One of my interns from the summer of 2006, Jesse, was coming out of high school and felt he was supposed to join the mission field. He decided to serve for three months in South Africa after graduating from high school. He went and served faithfully, but as he did, he ran into roadblocks along the way. Through it, he learned that he wasn't called to full-time missions, but rather to support, equip, and encourage those who are. He ended up studying at the University of Wisconsin – Madison and went on to hold sales and marketing positions at various companies. He is now a sales professional with IBM and is continuing to excel. He shared recently that going into his 2006 internship with me, he thought he was meant for the pulpit. Now, he and his wife not only support many missionaries personally, but he also serves as the chair for his church's mission and outreach program. He leads a team of 16 people and this program supports 20+ organizations with an incredibly large budget to spread the gospel and help those in need. Jesse has a drive and call to business *and also* to missions. Here's what is exciting: *one does not have to be at the expense of the other.*

Imagine if the God of the Universe created you specifically for the assignments he's given you. Imagine if when he breathed the breath of life into your lungs, he also anointed you for those assignments. Imagine if those unique giftings were hidden inside of you, waiting to be unlocked, understood, and released. I'm calling them forth. It's time for you to step into the fullness of what God created you to do. It's time for you to function full throttle in each of your anointings and advance the kingdom of God in supernatural ways. Don't miss a large portion of your assignment on earth because you spent your life trying to function in only one area when you were created to flourish in many.

That is the first part of David's life I felt the Holy Spirit leading me to study and teach the interns. Here is the second: Sometimes you will come up against opposition even before you stand in front of the giant.

If you want the full story, read 1 Samuel 15-17. I'm not a big detail guy, so here are the bullet points. David was diligently serving as a shepherd to his father's sheep when the Prophet Samuel anointed him to be the next King of Israel. It would be quite some time before he actually became king, and during this time, the Israelites were at war with the Philistines. David's father asked him to go check on his brothers in the battle and bring them some food. Upon arrival, he left his things with the keeper of supplies and ran to the battle line to meet his brothers. His oldest brother was angry when he saw him. He asked why he had come and with whom had he left his "few sheep." He criticized David's motive for being there and called him selfish, *"I know how conceited you are and how wicked your heart is."*[7] Can you imagine hearing that from your brother? This was his *family.* Someone on his team. His side of the battle. This was not a very warm family welcome – especially when you consider David was there in obedience to

---

[7] 1 Samuel 17:28 NIV

his father. Yet David didn't allow the criticism from his brother to stop him.

There will be times you have to persevere in the assignment God has placed on your life. You can be walking in obedience and still come up against opposition. Don't lose heart if this happens. If you are criticized, misunderstood, or demeaned – whether by the enemy or from those on your side, keep pressing on.

The story continues. David wanted to know what would be done for the "man who kills this Philistine and removes this disgrace from Israel? Who is this uncircumcised Philistine that he should defy the armies of the living God?"[8] King Saul caught wind of David asking questions around camp and sent for him. David offered to fight the giant himself and Saul replied, "You are not able to go out against this Philistine and fight him; you are only a young man, and he has been a warrior from his youth."[9]

You are not able.

Can you imagine hearing that from your leadership? Maybe you have. Perhaps you have encountered bad leadership where you were criticized or demeaned. Or it may be that you've had good leadership, but they misunderstood you or failed to recognize your calling. Consequently, they have not blessed and released you to function in your giftings. Take heart. You are in good company. Here's what we can learn from David's response to his situation:

---

[8] 1 Samuel 17:26 NIV

[9] 1 Samuel 17:33 NIV

1. Don't give up on what is in your heart.

David had been anointed. He had been trained. He had the Spirit of the Lord upon him. He had the heart of a warrior and he was walking in obedience. He didn't allow the fact that many didn't recognize all that was in him to stop him. David kept moving forward despite resistance, *but he did so with humility and honor.* This leads me to my next point:

2. Don't proceed until you have the blessing of your leadership.

David had such confidence in the power of God, and he understood that proper relation to authority is key to having influence in the kingdom of God. In humility, he explained to King Saul how he had been trained and what was in his heart to do. But he did not have a rebellious or critical attitude when doing so. He conveyed his giftings and it convinced Saul to say, "Go, and the Lord be with you."[10]

Many in our society today do not understand how to honor authority. We see dishonor and pride in the home between children and parents, in the workforce between employees and employers, and in how citizens relate to governmental authority. But allow me a moment to speak about pastoral authority within the church.

I'm more convinced than ever of what I said at the beginning of this book, "…advancing the kingdom of God is going to require all of us. Working together. As one body. With one mission. For the honor and the glory of Jesus' name."

TOGETHER.

Unity requires us to rightly relate to the leadership God has placed over us. Hebrews 13:17 says, "Obey your leaders and submit to them, for they are keeping watch over your souls, as those

---

[10] 1 Samuel 17:37 NIV

who will have to give an account. Let them do this with joy and not with groaning, for that would be of no advantage to you."

I strongly caution you to follow David's example when it comes to how you interact with pastoral authority within your local church. I've seen this handled poorly too many times. Some point of friction occurs, whether large or small, and a person decides, "Forget it. You don't understand me, Pastor. I'm just going to go do my own thing." When this happens, they are doing so *without* the blessing and cover of their pastoral leadership. This is not the way God has designed things to function and is a dangerous way to operate. Whatever is in their heart to do might start off strong, but after some time… maybe 6 months, maybe 36 months…it will blow up. It will end up doing more harm than good. And it is because they attempted to usurp Godly authority.

David could have bypassed the whole conversation with King Saul and run out to the giant and done his own thing. But he didn't. He waited for the blessing.[11] David understood Godly order and authority. He was honoring the God-ordained position of authority Saul held over him and, in doing so was honoring the Lord.

What if my leadership really is bad?

Most pastors genuinely have a heart that longs to obey the Lord and to help teach, shepherd and care for the children of God. Occasionally, there will be a pastor who is in disobedience before the Lord. Perhaps, like King Saul, they have allowed the fear of man or the opinion of others to knock them off track. Whatever the issue, their disobedience is between them and the Lord. Your response must still be honor. This is so countercultural! We must resolve not to allow offense, anger, bitterness, or resentment to take root in our hearts toward authority. In a day where the spirits

---

[11] If you are a pastor, please see my "Note to Pastors" in the appendix of this book

of rebellion and anarchy are on the move, choose to function in the opposite spirit. Choose to honor. Choose to submit. And watch what God does.

Here's my last bit of encouragement on that. If you are where God has called you and your leadership really is bad, the Lord will eventually either move your leader out of their position, or he will move you. Either way, it may not happen right away. It was many years before God moved King Saul out of his position of authority. But here's the key: during this whole time, David did not touch the Lord's anointed. He did not criticize. He did not rebel. He did not circumvent or usurp. And, he did not bail. The Lord saw that, and I believe it pleased his heart.

Most of you, like my interns, have giftings and anointings to function powerfully in many spheres of influence. But if you don't carry those with humility and honor, your impact will be severely limited.

CHAPTER 9

Epilogue

Have you ever been in a church service where the pastor calls a missionary who is about to be sent out to the mission field up to the front of the church? They have the other leaders in the church come up and surround this missionary. They lay hands on them and commission them to *go*. They pray over them, sometimes they anoint them. They pray for the blessing, protection, and favor of the Lord over them. The whole church is praying for them, hands extended.

Now picture this: What if a pastor called up the marketplace crowd – the businesspeople, the teachers, the dental hygienists, the students, the HR managers… and commissioned them in this same manner to go out into their mission fields and advance the Kingdom of God?

That would be powerful.

I've seen it happen. It *is* powerful.

Over the last few years, my pastor friend, Chris Conrad, and I have had the opportunity to speak in many different churches. And at the end of most of these services, we have an invitation for people to come forward and be prayed over. We specifically invite those who long to be used by God but are not in your traditional 'vocational ministry' roles. The *marketplace crowd*. A crowd whose sphere of influence is different from that of a missionary but whose call from Jesus to make disciples and share the love of Christ with those around them is just the same.

The pastor of the church hosting us joins Chris and me at the front. We extend the invitation, and do you know what? More often than not, nearly the **entire** church gets up to come forward.

Why? These people love God with all their hearts and long to serve Him, but they often don't quite know where they fit or how to do that in their lives outside of church. They haven't seen a model of how their unique giftings can be used in the body of Christ and therefore spend much time feeling their job is insignificant.

The enemy is feeding them a lie.

Are you believing that same lie?

Remember what I said in the introduction of this book?

"You're not second best. You were made to be children of the living God. Designed with intention and purpose. Created to seek and obey the will of your Father in heaven. Equipped to go out and bring the lost into His Kingdom. There are too many people out there – people who God loves, people Jesus died to save – who aren't going to walk into a church. But whether they know it yet or not, they are desperately searching for the truth. And He has positioned you in a specific arena to reach them."

When people come forward to be prayed over, we are simply blessing and validating the call that is on their lives. We are praying for the protection and favor of the Lord over them and *releasing them* to *go out*. They are receiving the blessing and commissioning from their pastoral leadership and the giftings on their lives are being fanned into flame.

Here's the key: This must be done in submission to your local pastor. The Lord is a God of order, submission, and authority – so what I'm NOT doing is telling you to march into your pastor's office and demand something. What I *am* saying is prayerfully consider sharing what has been stirring in your heart as you've read this book. In submission and honor, ask your pastor if they would consider having time in a service to do something like this – for you, and for your fellow believers like you.

And if you are a pastor yourself, prayerfully consider calling your congregation forward and *releasing them* to *go out*. To step confidently from that place of submission within their local church into their position in the body of Christ. From submission to their position. There is an army of believers waiting and longing to be validated in this way.

My fellow believer, your position is vitally important to the Kingdom. Do not let your position in the army of God go unoccupied by convincing yourself it doesn't matter. Advancing the Kingdom of God is going to require *all of us*. Working together. As one body. With one mission. For the honor and the glory of Jesus' name.

Will **You** Put Him First?

APPENDIX A

How to Share the Gospel

The most beautiful, powerful, and exhilarating thing I have the privilege of being a part of on this planet is seeing someone come to accept Jesus as their Lord. I'm telling you, *nothing* in this world comes *close* to that moment. I don't care how much money you have or how great your family is – it is an incomparable supernatural moment that changes someone's life for eternity. What I'd like to do over these next few pages is share with you some of my experiences in sharing the gospel with others. I'm not saying that the way I have done it is the way you should do it. Nor am I saying there is a formula that, if followed precisely, will result in someone's salvation. What I am saying is that the Bible tells us to "Always be prepared to give an answer to everyone who asks you to give the reason for the hope that you have."[12] And I want to share a little from my story in order to help you feel more prepared and comfortable when an opportunity to share the gospel presents itself. But please, take the pressure off yourself! Almost half of the New Testament in your Bible was written by the Apostle Paul – a guy who made clear he didn't come with "eloquence or human

---

[12] 1 Peter 3:15 NIV

wisdom as he proclaimed the testimony about God."[13] You can't save anyone anyway. Salvation is a work of God.

For those of you who have been present in the room when a baby is born, that is what leading someone to Christ can sometimes feel like. It is full of anticipation and excitement, but also nervousness and discomfort. Something truly special is about to take place, but someone needs to be in place to help deliver the baby. For a doctor who has studied and been trained to deliver babies, the idea of being in the room and helping deliver a baby is not intimidating. They know what to expect. They have gained knowledge and experience. And they had been in the delivery room many times with a more experienced doctor before they ever delivered a baby on their own. Now, contrast that doctor with a person who knows nothing about childbirth and has never been present for a live birth. Imagine the anxiety that person would feel if suddenly they were in a position where they had to deliver a baby. That sounds incredibly stressful to me. *Actually, it sounds a lot like the birth of my son, Teddy, who was just about born in the car on the way to the hospital. Don't worry though, we made it to the hospital and he waited a whole 6 minutes to make his grand entrance.*

That is why I want to try to give examples and help paint a picture for you of what it is like to lead someone to Christ. If you haven't done it yet, it can seem intimidating. Maybe you find yourself asking these questions: "What do I say? What if I don't know how to answer their questions? What if I say something wrong?" Believe me, we've all been there. And do you know what? There's no shame in not knowing the answer to a question! If... ok, *when*...I don't know how to answer a question someone brings up, I will simply tell them I don't know. I don't make something up. And then I'll say, "Let me take some time to study that for myself, or talk to someone I trust who knows the answer and get back to

---

[13] 1 Corinthians 2:1 NIV

you." Offering to connect them with someone like your pastor is a great option as well. That being said, it is incredible to me as I trust the Lord and am led by the Holy Spirit how often I will know the answer to a question someone might have. "But the Advocate, the Holy Spirit, whom the Father will send in my name, will teach you all things and will remind you of everything I have said to you."[14] Knowing I have the Holy Spirit inside of me guiding me gives me great peace and assurance.

Yes, leading someone to Christ for the first time can be intimidating, but once you know what's happening – and understand the miracle taking place – you will be eager to assist. I'm telling you, when the God of the universe lets you be the one to help deliver the person being 'born again'– just like the doctor does when a child is born – there is something extremely special about being 'in the room' at that moment. After all, it is part of your purpose here on earth.

Most of the opportunities I have had to lead people to the Lord have occurred just as I am going about my everyday life. At lunch, on a soccer field, in an interview, on a pool deck, on a golf course, with a building contractor discussing a future project, on a pier, in my office at work, and in a variety of "business meetings" over the years. Every person and situation is unique, but there are core biblical truths that have been present each time I have had a gospel-centered conversation with someone. They are as follows:

#1 We've all sinned. Somewhere in the story, this *has* to be said. I mean, you know you've sinned, don't you? I know I have. We've all sinned and we've all fallen short of the glory of God.[15] Our sin is what separates us from a Holy God… from a right relationship with Him.

---

[14] John 14:26 NIV

[15] Romans 3:23 NIV

#2 God loves us and made a way. "For God so loved the world that he gave his one and only Son, that whoever believes in him shall not perish but have eternal life."[16] God "so loved the world…" because "God *is* love."[17] The love that he has for us is so much greater than we could ever imagine. Jesus loved us so much that he died on the cross in our place. He took the punishment of our sins on himself so that we could have eternal life.

#3 God is offering to adopt us. "For he chose us in him before the creation of the world to be holy and blameless in his sight. In love he predestined us for adoption to sonship through Jesus Christ, in accordance with his pleasure and will…"[18] He wants us to be a part of his family – for all eternity.

#4 Believe and confess. "If you declare with your mouth, "Jesus is Lord," and believe in your heart that God raised him from the dead, you will be saved. For it is with your heart that you believe and are justified, and it is with your mouth that you profess your faith and are saved."[19] He's not waiting for you to get your act together before you come to him. His heart desires that you and I say "yes" to him today.

There are times I will quote an exact reference, but other times I will simply allude to the principle or truth in those scriptures. I'm a storyteller, so this way comes naturally to me. As the conversation develops, I stay attentive to what I sense the Holy Spirit is saying at that moment.

---

[16] John 3:16 NIV

[17] 1 John 4:8 NIV

[18] Ephesians 1:4-5 NIV

[19] Romans 10:9-10 NIV

Let me pause right there. This does not mean I hear God audibly. Some people have heard God in that way, but that hasn't been the case for me nor is it for most people. If you read the chapters before this, you heard me describe hearing God as more of a *knowing* or a *sense...* somewhere between my chest and belly button. That's what I'm talking about here when I say I stay attentive to what I sense the Holy Spirit saying.

Most of the time as I am talking, there will come a moment where I will say one word or sentence that will just foundationally touch me. It's hard to describe, but I will know immediately: *this word is what this conversation is going to be about.* This happens almost every single time for me.

My brother Ted has led a lot of people to Christ, and one time he told me that in the midst of doing so, he asks God: "Tell me what the one word is… what's the on-ramp for this person?" Ted said to me, "You know, the woman at the well received one word from Jesus Christ – and the entire village got saved." So as I'm talking with someone about salvation, I'm asking the Lord, "What is the on-ramp for this person? What is the one word – the route this person can relate to?" It is amazing to me how personal God is. He knows people so well and knows the exact word that person needs to hear to unlock their heart. When that moment happens, I can see it in them. Something inside of them shifts. I can tell they are engaged with what is being said.

Here's where it gets really exciting. A lot of times as that moment of salvation draws near, I will start to have tears come to my eyes. When this happens to me, I know that person is about to accept Christ. They are about to be born again. And at that point, I never stop. I don't care if the room blows up, I stay focused.

There are two things I mention before I transition into asking them if they'd like to make a decision to accept Christ:

1) I make sure to convey *Who* they are accepting. I briefly mention that Jesus is the perfect Savior, that God is a loving Father, and that the Holy Spirit is our advocate and teacher. God is pure and holy and good. All he wants for them is the best. THAT is who they are inviting in. Some people have an inaccurate representation in their mind of who God is and that can cause a big hurdle for them when it comes to spiritual conversation.
2) I make it very clear that Jesus is the *only way* to a relationship with God the Father. If there were any other way, it would be cruel of God to make his one and only Son die the death he did on our behalf. Because of the blood Jesus shed for you and me, we have the right to become children of God. Amazing.

At this point in the conversation, I present an invitation. I'll say something like, "You know, in the Bible, it says that Jesus stands at the door (of our hearts) and knocks – and that if we decide to open the door, he will come in."[20] It is not uncommon for the person I'm talking with to physically feel their heart pounding at this moment. This doesn't always happen, but I have often had people tell me after they accept Christ: "When you were talking about accepting Christ, my heart was pounding out of my chest!" I believe this is the Holy Spirit reaching out to their heart, knocking and saying, "Come be with me, I want you."

There's something about the tension of this moment. You have to give them a chance to respond. Through a lot of this conversation, you've been sharing some of your story and perhaps some bible verses, but there comes a point where the ball has to be put in their court. Sometimes I'll say something like, "When I gave my life to Christ, someone helped lead me in a prayer. We prayed

---

[20] See Revelation 3:20

something like this..." I will then continue on and simply go through an example of a basic prayer of salvation. Nothing fancy or long.[21] I will then say something like, "You know, this moment is not so much about the exact words we say. The key is that in your heart, you are responding and deciding to open the door for Jesus Christ to come in. Then I will pause before continuing, "If *you're* at the point where *you* want to move forward and accept Christ, I'd be happy to lead you in that prayer right now."

One thing to keep in mind here is that God gives us free will. He will not open the door. I make a point to convey this is their decision as to whether they will open the door or not. Most of the time, if the conversation has gone this far, the person is ready to accept Christ. But that is not always the case. This is very important: If they are not quite there yet, you must honor that. This is between them and God. You're not trying to get them to buy something. You're simply providing an invitation. Remember, *you* can't save anyone. Salvation is a work of God.

If they say, "Not today," that's ok! You have planted a seed, and the Holy Spirit will continue to water the "soil" of their heart. But in my experience, the vast majority of the time, the person says, "Yes."

When that happens, I remind them what Romans 10 says: "... declare with your mouth, "Jesus is Lord," and believe in your heart that God raised him from the dead..." Sometimes I will join hands with them and then we'll bow our heads together. I'll say, "How about you repeat after me?"... and we'll pray something like this:

"Dear God, I'm so sorry that I've sinned. I know I'm a sinner. And I know that I can't pay the price for my sins to be forgiven. But I believe that when Jesus died on the cross, he died for my sins. I believe that He was resurrected from death... and today, I accept

---

[21] See example in a few paragraphs

Jesus Christ as my Lord and my Savior. I want to be adopted into your family. And I ask that to be sealed right now in Jesus' name."

At that moment, rejoicing begins in heaven.[22] It is a holy moment. Don't rush it. What just took place was supernatural and life-changing. Lingering is ok. There have been times I've been with people who begin to cry or laugh. I've also had times where we just sat in silence in the presence of the Lord. Consistently, people describe feeling very light and peaceful.

One thing that is interesting is people are often struck by how easy it was. We are so wired to try to earn things. Salvation does not work that way. The work has already been done. The price already paid on the cross. All that is left is for us to receive.

As we wrap up our time together, I will affirm the decision they just made. I tell them that what they just did will change their life. And I encourage them to tell someone else about the decision they just made – maybe a spouse, friend, or pastor. This helps solidify in them what has just taken place.

Then I leave them with this truth based upon their decision to open the door of their heart…

You are now a child of the living God.

Jesus describes himself in the Bible as the "Good Shepherd." He says in John 10:3-4 ESV, "The sheep hear his voice, and he calls his own sheep by name and leads them out. When he has brought out all his own, he goes before them, and the sheep follow him, for they know his voice." Never forget that verse. You can hear your Father's voice. Don't ever allow anyone or anything to tell you differently. You were created to hear him speak. He's calling you by name. **You. Are. His.**

---

[22] Luke 15:10 NIV

The Gospel Blueprint

The Bible tells us that Jesus stands at the door and knocks, but it is up to us to open the door. Is he knocking on the door of your heart right now? Do you know *about* Jesus, but aren't sure that you have been *born again?*

We were made for a relationship with God, but our own sin has gotten in the way.

> **Romans 3:23** "All have sinned and fall short of the glory of God."

Because of our own sin, what we deserve is death (aka 'eternal separation from God')

> **Isaiah 59:2** "But your iniquities have separated you from your God; your sins have hidden his face from you, so that he will not hear."

Sin separates us from a holy God and death is what we deserve...

> **Romans 6:23a** "The wages of sin is death..."

But God in His great mercy offers us something stunning.

> **Romans 6:23b** "...but the free gift of God is eternal life in Christ Jesus our Lord."

This means we can stop striving. Stop trying to *earn* our salvation through our 'good works' because our efforts will always be in vain. No matter how hard we try, we can never measure up to God's level of perfection.

Ephesians 2:8-9 "For it is by grace you have been saved, through faith—and this is not from yourselves, it is the gift of God—not by works, so that no one can boast."

When we are given a gift, all we have to do is *receive* it.

John 1:12 "But as many as received Him, to them He gave the right to become children of God, *even* to those who believe in His name…"

When we hear his word, we simply must believe. That's the key to avoiding eternal separation from God.

John 5:24 "Truly, truly, I say to you, he who hears My word, and believes Him who sent Me, has eternal life, and does not come into judgment, but has passed out of death into life."

Jesus paid the price that we could never pay on our own. He was a perfect sacrifice on our behalf.

1 Peter 3:18 "For Christ also died for sins once for all, the just for the unjust, so that He might bring us to God, having been put to death in the flesh, but made alive in the spirit;"

And whether we choose to open the door of our hearts and receive his gift is up to us.

Revelation 3:20 "Behold, I stand at the door and knock; if anyone hears My voice and opens the door, I will come in to him and will dine with him, and he with Me."

We have to open the door. Jesus is the *only way* to have a relationship with God the Father. If there were any other way, it would be cruel of God to make his one and only Son die the death he did on our behalf. Because of the blood Jesus shed for us, we have the right to become children of God. Amazing.

Are you ready to open the door of your heart?

> **Romans 10:9-10** "If you declare with your mouth, "Jesus is Lord," and believe in your heart that God raised him from the dead, you will be saved. For it is with your heart that you believe and are justified, and it is with your mouth that you profess your faith and are saved."

Follow-Up

If you just prayed that prayer for the first time, you have been born again and all of heaven is rejoicing. You have been given a new heart…

> **Ezekiel 36:26** "Moreover, I will give you a new heart and put a new spirit within you; and I will remove the heart of stone from your flesh and give you a heart of flesh."

You are a new creation. Your life on earth and for all of eternity will never be the same. And now, you have an invitation from God to approach his throne – not as a servant, but as *His child*.

> **Romans 8:14-17** "For those who are led by the Spirit of God are the children of God. The Spirit you received does not make you slaves, so that you live in fear again; rather, the Spirit you received brought about your adoption to sonship. And by him we cry, *"Abba,* Father." The Spirit himself testifies with our spirit that we are God's children.

Now if we are children, then we are heirs—heirs of God and co-heirs with Christ, if indeed we share in his sufferings in order that we may also share in his glory."

If you just accepted Jesus' invitation and surrendered your life to him, we would love to celebrate with you! Email us and let us know at info@willyouputmefirst.com and we will send you a gift to help you on your journey with Jesus.

APPENDIX B

Hearing the Voice of God

I have shared these stories with many people over the years and a common response when I finish is this: "That's really cool, but what does it look like to put God first in *my* job?" The simple answer is that it looks different for each one of us, but in *every* situation, it always boils down to one thing: *obedience.* Obedience to God is the key to a truly successful life. And we can't learn to obey him if we don't know what he is saying. We need to know the Word of God and we need to know His voice. Jesus says, "My sheep hear my voice, and I know them, and they follow me."[23] I love how Jesus used metaphors to simplify things when he taught. Hearing God does not require years of study in seminary or the title of pastor. Those are both great, but what is required to hear God is simply a *relationship* with Him. Jesus says that in order to have this relationship and to see the Kingdom of God, we must be born again.[24] This is not a physical rebirth, but rather a spiritual one. When we believe in the name of Jesus for the forgiveness of

---

[23] John 10:27 ESV
[24] John 3:3 NIV

our sins, he gives us a new heart.[25] At that moment, the Holy Spirit takes up residence[26] inside us and we are granted *access* to God.[27] We become children of God.[28] That's stunning!

Let me tell a quick story to illustrate the significance of being a child. The Princeton Club offers free childcare so parents can drop off their kids to play while they work out. When my kids were younger, there were times I would bring them to work with me and they loved going into the playroom to play with their friends. When it was time to head home, I would make my way over to the playroom and call for Teddy and Jessie by name. Being that I worked at the club and was around often, a lot of the kids knew who I was. I've been known to give a kid a sweet treat upon meeting them – something I do to this day. M&M's are a sure way to make a kid smile. So, when it was time for me to take my kids home, several of the other children in the playroom would come rushing to the door. I would smile and say hello while making a couple of them jump to give me a high five. But the only kids I left that room with were my own. It's not that I didn't like the other kids… it's not even that I wasn't familiar with them – it's simply that they were not my kids. Being familiar with someone and being their child are two very different things. It's the exact same with God. You can know about Jesus, and you might even be familiar with the things of God… but until you are born again – that is, until you accept the free gift of salvation, you have not yet been adopted into the family of God. And without being his child, it's hard to hear his voice.

I've never heard God audibly. Some people do hear God this way, but that is not the case for most. As you've read in the earlier stories, I describe hearing God as more of a *knowing* or a *sense*…

---

[25] Ezekiel 36:26 NIV

[26] 1 Corinthians 3:16 NIV

[27] Ephesians 2:18; 3:12 NIV

[28] John 1:12 NIV

somewhere between my chest and belly button. Before you go down the road of thinking I'm a nut job (*maybe you already have*) let me explain something:

Each of us is a 3-part being. Every human being is made up of a body, soul, and spirit. 1 Thessalonians 5:23 distinguishes the three by addressing each: "May God himself, the God of peace, sanctify you through and through. May your whole *spirit, soul* and *body* be kept blameless at the coming of our Lord Jesus Christ." Each part has its own purpose.

- Our **BODY** is the *physical* part. Think about our five senses: human beings can see, hear, taste, touch, and smell. Our body is the structure that holds our soul and spirit. This is the part you see when you look in the mirror.
- Our **SOUL** is our *mind, will, and emotions*. We don't *have* a soul as much as we *are* a soul. It's the core of our being and personality.
- Our **SPIRIT** is our *essence* or *life*. Like the soul, our spirit has no physical aspect, so it can't be seen. It's the breath that God breathed into Adam, and what leaves us at our earthly death.

So, if "God is Spirit,"[29] and we have a spirit, doesn't it make sense that he would communicate with us Spirit to spirit? In order for this to happen, though, our spirit must be *made new*. God tells us in the Old Testament how this works: "Moreover, I will give you a new heart and put a new spirit within you; and I will remove the heart of stone from your flesh and give you a heart of flesh."[30] But in order for this great exchange to take place, we must be *in Christ*. We must choose to have a *relationship* with him.

---

[29] John 4:24 NLT

[30] Ezekiel 36:26 NASB

"Therefore, if anyone is in Christ, he is a new creation. The old has passed away; behold, the new has come."[31]

If you are in a relationship with Christ, you already have the ability to hear God. Did you catch that? *You already have the ability to hear God.* You may have doubted it or not have actively practiced hearing God – but make no mistake – you can hear your Father's voice. He chooses to speak to us today through the Bible, other people, circumstances, and directly to our spirit, but don't miss this profound and simple truth: once you enter into a relationship with Jesus Christ, you can hear God.

Here's a simple checklist to keep in mind when it comes to hearing the voice of the Lord:

No contradiction. No condemnation. No conformity.

- **No CONTRADICTION.** If you ever think you are hearing something from the Lord and it does not align with his written word, it is not from him. PERIOD. "For God is not a God of confusion but of peace."[32] "God is not man, that he should lie, or a son of man, that he should change his mind. Has he said, and will he not do it? Or has he spoken, and will he not fulfill it?"[33] God's voice always aligns with what he has spoken in the past.
- **No CONDEMNATION.** The voice of the Lord will never be shaming or condemning. He may bring conviction or rebuke, but that is done in love. If the voice you're hearing is heaping shame on you, be assured it is not the voice of your

---

[31] 2 Corinthians 5:17 ESV
[32] 1 Corinthians 14:33 NASB
[33] Numbers 23:19 ESV

heavenly Father. "Therefore, there is now no condemnation for those who are in Christ Jesus."[34]

- **No CONFORMITY.** The Kingdom of God is full of truths that oppose what our culture tells us. Here are a few examples: "So the last will be first, and the first will be last."[35] "For whoever wants to save their life will lose it, but whoever loses their life for me will find it."[36] "Do not conform to the pattern of this world, but be transformed by the renewing of your mind. Then you will be able to test and approve what God's will is—his good, pleasing and perfect will."[37] Similarly, the voice of God will never conform to the pattern, trends, or fads of the world.

Remember, once you enter into a relationship with Jesus Christ, you can hear God. Find a quiet place, still your mind, and pay attention to that *sense* or *knowing* from God. You might even hear Him somewhere between your chest and your belly button.

---

[34] Romans 8:1 NIV
[35] Matthew 20:16 NIV
[36] Matthew 16:25 NIV
[37] Romans 12:2 NIV

APPENDIX C

A Note To Pastors

Dear Pastor,

I. AM. SO. FOR. YOU. You need to hear me say that because you don't know me and may understandably be skeptical of a guy like me telling stories to inspire your congregation to suit up and step into their role outside of the four walls of the church. Allow me to share something with you. For the better part of the last 2 decades, the Lord has allowed me to walk alongside a number of amazing pastors. Part of what my wife and I feel called to do is host pastors and their families in our homes. We even built the home we currently live in as a pastoral retreat center. It was created to provide a place of rest and refreshment for those on the frontlines in ministry.

At times, that looks like having a pastor and his whole family stay with us for a week to have a vacation, to let their guard down and relax, enjoying fun activities and time with their loved ones. Other times we'll leave and allow them to have the whole place to themselves. But our family's favorite is when we host a group of 10 pastors for a 2- or 3-day retreat. I'm not joking. I get to encourage them with stories. My wife prepares amazing meals. My kids come around to help serve and share their own stories, and even my siblings come to pray for and minister to the pastors. I know it is part of my assignment on earth, and I am passionate about it.

Why does this matter? Because you need it. It's likely that you are carrying way too much stress and weight on yourself. I empathize with that burden. All too often, you are doing all of the lifting by yourself and you shouldn't have to. In my close relationships with pastors over the years, I have observed that often the reason they are so exhausted is that there are a lot of people like me who are supposed to carry the load in the body of Christ, and we are not doing our part. I believe what the Lord is doing right now is raising up an army of believers to help shoulder the load you've been single-handedly carrying. I believe he wants us to carry it **together**. If you keep carrying it all on your own, I think there's a high likelihood you will experience burnout.

For years, I've had this sense that there are many people like me sitting in the pews week after week unsure of our role in the army of God. What I mean by that is, just as you were created by God to lead a body of believers, we were created by God to **be sent by you** to serve outside of the four walls and see His Kingdom expand in those places. I want to do it with your blessing.

That's why I want to encourage you to lay your hands on people like me and, in the authority of Jesus Christ, commission them to run the race they were made to run. Help them see they were made differently than you and how that is a good thing.

Join me in having the faith to trust the Lord to be the head of His church. In your case, I think this will enable you to delegate responsibility and bring freedom to your life. Rest in knowing your Heavenly Father is Lord over His kingdom – and that His kingdom is so much bigger than one local church. Trust Him.

Equip, bless and commission the businessperson in your church – with all the connections and relationships with the marketing companies, tv stations, and banks – to head up a campaign in your city to feed the hungry.

Equip, bless and commission the nurse in your church to really understand that her role in loving and caring for the health of those in need is holy and needed to make the body of Christ whole.

Equip, bless and commission the young entrepreneur in your church. Help them to understand the importance of their idea and their value in bringing the Kingdom of God into that market. Fan into flame the gift of God in their lives and watch them revolutionize an industry – for the honor and glory of the name of Jesus.

Equip, bless and commission the young mom in your church who has a heart to build relationships with other young moms in the community. Don't make her feel obligated to run the church nursery if that's not where she feels called. Fuel her desire to make her home a safe place for other moms to come, build relationships, make meals, encourage one another, share the load, and show the love of Jesus – right out in her community.

Don't make these people feel pressure or guilt to fill a certain role only within the church building. Take the top off of what we've traditionally called ministry and just watch what God is going to do. My friend Chris (a pastor) says it this way, "Release people into the marketplace instead of trying to get them to be greeters or get them to serve on the board. Instead, recognize they have an actual apostolic anointing on them and release them into the calling God has for them in the marketplace. When we do this, we will watch Holy Spirit do amazing work in the marketplace through them that we could never do."

Rest assured, I am not the guy who is disgruntled with the church. I believe in the local church. I am for unity in the body of Christ. I am submitted to my local pastor. And I don't have a critical spirit towards you or your role.

I honor you and the battle you are fighting, the love you are pouring out on the bride of Christ, and the shepherding and teaching you are doing to care for His people. You are amazing and I am so thankful for you. I could not do what you do. In fact, that's actually the bottom line: I can't do what you do. You can't do what I do. **We need each other**. Advancing the kingdom of God is going to require all of us. Working together. As one body. With one mission. For the honor and the glory of the name Jesus.

— Dave

If you are interested in inviting Dave to speak to your group, email us: info@willyouputmefirst.com

Visit willyouputmefirst.com for more information:

Printed in the USA
CPSIA information can be obtained
at www.ICGtesting.com
CBHW051927101123
1743CB00002B/6